A Report by a Panel of the

NATIONAL ACADEMY OF
PUBLIC ADMINISTRATION

for the United States Environmental Protection Agency

December 2001

ENVIRONMENTAL JUSTICE IN EPA PERMITTING: REDUCING POLLUTION IN HIGH-RISK COMMUNITIES IS INTEGRAL TO THE AGENCY'S MISSION

Panel
Philip Rutledge, *Chair*
James Barnes
Jonathan Howes
Valerie Lemmie
James Mora
James Murley
Eddie Williams

The views in this document are those of the Panel alone. They do not necessarily reflect the views of the Academy as an institution.

This document was funded by the U.S. Environmental Protection Agency Cooperative Agreement Number EQ-82906401-0.

Academy Project Number 1969

TABLE OF CONTENTS

CHAPTER 5 – EQUIPPING COMMUNITIES AND EPA STAFF FOR BETTER PUBLIC PARTICIPATION IN PERMITTING

APPENDICES

BIBLIOGRAPHY

ADDITIONAL RESOURCES

FOREWORD

Like efficiency and economy, social equity is integral to the effective administration of public policies and programs. The National Academy of Public Administration (the Academy) believes that social equity issues represent a central element of its work in this new century and a critical aspect in delivering public services for this country. In February 2000, the Academy's Board of Trustees created the Standing Panel on Social Equity in Governance. The Standing Panel defines social equity as, "the fair, just and equitable management of all institutions serving the public directly or by contract and the fair, just and equitable distribution of public services and implementation of public policy." Among its goals is to "review and evaluate developments in public administration that have to do with critical matters in social equity."

This report, "Environmental Justice in EPA Permitting: Reducing Pollution in High-Risk Communities Is Integral to the Agency's Mission," is the Standing Panel's first research and evaluation project since the creation of the Academy's Standing Panel. It represents an important opportunity for the Panel members to assess the efforts of the U.S. Environmental Protection Agency (EPA) in addressing the widely recognized fact that some low-income and people of color communities are exposed to significantly greater environmental and public health hazards than other communities. This report is designed to help those community members and other stakeholders gain a better understanding of how they can more effectively bring environmental justice concerns to the attention of EPA's permitting programs.

The Academy's Panel for this project recommends changes to EPA in four distinct areas of environmental justice: leadership, permitting procedures, priority setting, and public participation.

> **Leadership.** The Panel recommends that EPA build on the solid policy foundation underlying its environmental justice programs to ensure that these considerations are integrated into the agency's core mission. This change will require sustained leadership, clearer performance goals, improved outcome measures, stronger accountability mechanisms, and better training.

> **Permitting Procedures.** The Panel recommends that EPA use fully its existing legal authorities to ensure that its permitting programs can more effectively address environmental justice concerns. EPA should provide simpler tools that enable permit writers to identify and address exposures in high-risk communities, expand monitoring to provide these writers with better information, and focus more enforcement resources on communities that are disproportionately impacted by pollution.

Priority Setting. The Panel recommends that EPA work with state and local authorities to identify high-risk communities and prioritize them for pollution reduction efforts using various tools, including the permitting process.

Public Participation. Public participation is critical to a credible permitting program. The Panel recommends that EPA provide more resources to aid participation by historically underrepresented groups, create new opportunities for them to participate earlier in the process, and use informal dispute resolution processes more frequently.

The Academy hopes that this study will contribute to a better public understanding of how EPA can more effectively address environmental justice concerns in its permitting programs. At the same time, it understands that states carry out most environmental permitting. This report, combined with the Academy's next project which will examine how some states deal with environmental justice issues, should provide the public and states with additional information about how permitting practices and related programs can be improved so they better address environmental justice concerns.

In conducting this study, the Academy Panel has received excellent assistance from EPA headquarters and regional officials, as well as from representatives of community groups, regulated industry, and state environmental agencies. We are most grateful to all those interviewed who so generously contributed their time and views to help the staff conduct this study. We are also grateful to EPA's Office of Environmental Justice for its financial support and to our Panel members who worked diligently to produce this report.

Robert J. O'Neill, Jr.
President
National Academy of Public Administration

EXECUTIVE SUMMARY

The Office of Environmental Justice at the U.S. Environmental Protection Agency (EPA) in June 2001 asked the National Academy of Public Administration (the Academy) to study EPA's programs for issuing air, water, and waste permits. The project's goal is to determine how environmental justice could be incorporated into these three permitting programs as a practical matter of public administration. The study is also designed to contribute to the Office's five-step strategy for integrating environmental justice into EPA's permitting processes. The five steps are seeking advice and recommendations on the issue, securing legal and administrative analyses, developing training, ensuring implementation, and assessing results.

As defined by EPA,

> Environmental Justice is the fair treatment and meaningful involvement of all people regardless of race, color, national origin, culture, education, or income with respect to the development, implementation, and enforcement of environmental laws, regulations, and policies. *Fair treatment* means that no group of people, including racial, ethnic, or socioeconomic groups, should bear a disproportionate share of the negative consequences resulting from industrial, municipal, and commercial operations or the execution of federal, state, local, and tribal environmental programs and policies. *Meaningful involvement* means that: (1) potentially affected community residents have an appropriate opportunity to participate in decisions about a proposed activity that will affect their environment and/or health; (2) the public's contribution can influence the regulatory agency's decision; (3) the concerns of all participants involved will be considered in the decision-making process; and (4) the decision-makers seek out and facilitate the involvement of those potentially affected.[1]

This Academy study is intended to help the public better understand how EPA can incorporate environmental justice concerns into its permitting programs under existing legal authorities contained in the Clean Air Act, the Clean Water Act, and the Resource Conservation and Recovery Act. The Academy Panel has recommended improvements to the agency's efforts to address environmental justice through its site-specific permits. It also has examined ways for EPA to reinforce these efforts through:

- strengthening leadership
- better integrating environmental justice into its core mission
- improving the training and tools made available to permit writers
- increasing permit writers' awareness of environmental justice concerns and what can be done about them
- identifying high-risk communities so the agency can focus its limited resources on the highest priority problems
- improving monitoring to identify emissions that cause the most concern

1

- increasing the resources available for communities to participate in the permitting process
- providing more timely public notice of permit applications
- working more closely with communities
- using neutral third parties more frequently to facilitate dialogues about disputed permits

The Academy's Panel has found that EPA's environmental justice efforts need to be better integrated into all of its programs and implemented as part of the agency's core mission. Like prior Academy studies,[2] this report stresses that EPA should establish clear accountability for results and use appropriate public administration techniques to ensure that its managers and staff are receptive to, and willing to execute fully, their responsibilities for achieving environmental justice.

COMPLETE FINDINGS

Finding 1: EPA's leadership has articulated a clear commitment to environmental justice that predates the 1994 Executive Order and continues into the current administration.

Finding 2: Despite the commitment of senior EPA leadership, environmental justice has not yet been integrated fully into the agency's core mission or its staff functions. Expectations for specific outcomes have not accompanied these commitments, nor has the agency adopted methods for measuring progress in achieving them or accountability to ensure that EPA managers and staff work toward implementing environmental justice policies.

Finding 3: EPA has significant statutory and regulatory authority, as well as numerous opportunities for exercising discretion, to incorporate environmental justice considerations into its air, water, and waste permitting programs.

Finding 4: The existing agency culture is one barrier to incorporating environmental justice into EPA's permitting programs. This culture does not treat environmental justice as a central element of the agency's core programs.

Finding 5: A recent General Counsel's legal opinion makes it clear that the Clean Air Act, Clean Water Act, and Resource Recovery and Conservation Act provide ample authority for EPA's permitting staff to address high-risk community concerns when developing the terms and conditions of individual facility permits. EPA Administrator Christine Todd Whitman has reaffirmed this opinion in her August 9, 2001 memorandum to senior EPA officials.[3]

Finding 6: EPA managers have not routinely provided straightforward, practical tools and procedures to their permitting staff for incorporating community concerns into permits, nor have they directed the staff to ensure that environmental justice concerns are systematically considered in EPA's permitting programs.

Finding 7: Many EPA permit writers have not had an opportunity to learn how they can contribute to resolving environmental justice concerns by obtaining more information about the community that may be affected by a proposed permit; the nature of the risks that the community faces; community concerns related to the proposed facility; the community's capacity to participate in the permitting process; and the best methods for communicating with the community.

Finding 8: Given that its legal authority to issue permits for particular facilities is based on the Clean Air Act, Clean Water Act and Resource Recovery and Conservation Act, EPA has limited ability to deal with other common concerns in high-risk communities, such as noise, traffic, and odor.

Finding 9: EPA's credibility relating to permitting programs in high-risk communities depends upon timely and rigorous review of permit renewals for existing facilities and on using opportunities to enforce visibly their permit conditions, including increased inspections and local monitoring of environmental conditions.

Finding 10: EPA does not now have a routine process for identifying high-risk communities and giving them priority attention to prevent pollution and reduce existing public health hazards.

Finding 11: Many parties support the need for EPA to conduct cumulative risk assessments when evaluating permit applications, but the current state of this science has not advanced sufficiently to conduct these assessments. However, EPA has efforts underway to improve the science so that it will be more feasible and practical. While waiting for cumulative risk assessment science to advance, EPA, several states, and citizen groups have developed and applied other tools that analyze exposures of disproportionately impacted communities to actual or potential amounts of multiple pollutants. More frequent and comprehensive environmental monitoring in these communities can help EPA to determine whether they need priority attention.

Finding 12: Limited environmental data, and their lack of accuracy, are barriers to risk reduction, particularly when analyzing very localized, community-level environmental conditions and impacts.

Finding 13: Absent a consistent, national approach for assessing risks, several EPA regional offices have developed tools for evaluating disproportionate impacts from pollution. These tools, combined with EPA regional experiences, have created an important body of practical experience. Yet, EPA has not evaluated or catalogued them so that the agency's permitting programs can learn about best practices, the elements needed to develop a national guidance document on analyzing cumulative risks, or any potential concerns about the scientific validity of the tools.

Finding 14: Many government officials, business representatives, and community activists believe that EPA's formal avenues for public participation in the permitting process are inadequate to address the concerns of disproportionately impacted communities. The public remains uninvolved until EPA has negotiated with applicants and resolved most of the permit questions.

Finding 15: To have a more effective voice in permit decisions, community group members need better training on how to participate in the process, resources to obtain technical help for more effective participation, and earlier notice about the proposed permit application. The last would allow them to become involved in negotiations with the applicant at the same time as EPA.

Finding 16: EPA has experimented with various ways of enhancing public participation, but these techniques are not yet standard operating procedure for the agency's permitting processes in the air, water, and waste programs.

Finding 17: Facilitated dialogues, using well-trained neutral third parties, can make significant contributions to resolving many community concerns about permitting, especially if they are conducted very early in the process.

Finding 18: Giving early notice to local officials about permit applications can enable them to consider such community concerns as odor, noise, traffic, and other issues that are outside EPA's jurisdiction, but that local agencies may have authority to address.

Finding 19: EPA technical assistance and facilitated dialogue resources for community groups regarding permitting are quite limited except in the Superfund program.

Finding 20: Disproportionately impacted community members want better access to technical information that will enable them to participate more effectively in negotiations about permit terms and conditions.

COMPLETE RECOMMENDATIONS

Chapter 2

- Building on Administrator Whitman's recent environmental justice memorandum, the Assistant Administrators for Air, Water, and Waste, and the Regional Administrators should reinforce the importance of this policy, its role in implementing EPA's core mission, and the expectation that their managers and staff will implement environmental justice in their projects and activities.

- EPA should finalize its draft national environmental justice guidance and develop practical tools for permit writers to identify and address environmental justice issues arising in air, water, and waste permits.

- The Offices of Air, Water, and Waste should develop strategic plans demonstrating how environmental justice will be integrated into the substance and procedures of their permitting programs, and they should carefully examine how they can use the authorities set forth in the General Counsel's legal opinion dated December 1, 2001, to incorporate environmental justice concerns into permits for new and ongoing projects.

- Each office's plan for incorporating environmental justice in its permitting programs should include goals, measures of performance, expected outcomes, accountability mechanisms, and time frames for meeting the goals.

- EPA should establish an accountability process that includes clear performance measures for evaluating how well employees – both managers and staff – are able to incorporate environmental justice into air, water, and waste permits.

- EPA should identify disproportionately impacted and other adversely affected communities and establish explicit goals for reducing risks there. The agency should set clear expectations for producing results that are directly linked to the agency's mission and give staff an important performance measure that they can support in a whole-hearted fashion. These tasks could also provide measures of EPA's progress in implementing environmental justice and could be reinforced by agency-wide reporting that tracks their progress.

- EPA should develop a communication mechanism for sharing information with all air, water and waste programs, regional offices, and states about effective tools for addressing environmental justice, including descriptions of best practices and lessons learned. This mechanism should coordinate EPA's activities for incorporating environmental justice into permitting, so that permit writers in all the air, water, and waste programs and regional offices can become more effective and gain greater efficiency and effectiveness in responding to environmental justice concerns.

- EPA should evaluate the effectiveness of its national workshop on the Fundamentals of Environmental Justice to determine how well it meets its intended objectives, including the effective implementation of environmental justice in permitting.

- EPA should develop a program for rewarding employees' extra efforts to address environmental justice in permitting, through recognition in existing national awards and development of headquarters and regional office recognition programs.

Chapter 3

- In the short-term, EPA should determine whether it can provide communities with earlier notice of permit applications, at least as soon as agency staff determine the applications to be complete. This would provide more opportunities for the public to interact directly with the agency's permit writers and allow consideration of community information and concerns during the drafting and negotiation stages.

- In the long-term, EPA should revise its permitting regulations to ensure that nearby communities are notified of a permit application as early as possible, and certainly as soon as the application is complete.

- EPA should revise its public notification practices to ensure that notices are provided in languages common to affected communities and placed at libraries, churches, community centers, and other locations where many community residents can see them.

- EPA managers should provide their permit writers with checklists or similar tools, to aid them in identifying and considering potential environmental justice concerns.

- EPA budget and administrative staff should recognize the additional time and effort that permit writers need to develop permit conditions for environmental justice issues and to work more closely with community groups. They should adjust the agency's workload models as appropriate to determine the average number of permits that each writer is expected to handle.

- EPA's air, water, and waste programs should ensure that their permits fully implement current environmental standards and should modify or add standards, if necessary, to ensure that pollution levels are reduced to better protect public health.

- EPA's air, water, and waste programs should place high priority on the elimination of permit renewal backlogs to ensure that facilities have conditions that are as up-to-date and protective as possible, especially for those affecting high-risk or disproportionately impacted communities.

- EPA's air, water, and waste programs should develop specific guidance documents on the legal requirements and discretionary authorities that permit writers have to require additional monitoring and public reporting in disproportionately impacted communities.

- EPA should consider using facilitated dialogues as part of its permitting process, at least in some cases, by creating and utilizing a decision-tree approach. This approach could help to incorporate environmental justice concerns in EPA permits by: (1) preparing permit conditions that address community concerns; (2) facilitating interactions between permit applicants and affected residents; (3) providing an opportunity for local authorities to address such issues as noise, odor, and traffic that EPA cannot resolve; and (4) crafting voluntary agreements among permit applicants, the community, EPA, and relevant state or local agencies.

- EPA's Office of Enforcement and Compliance Assurance (OECA) should use environmental justice as a criterion for deciding the locations and types of facilities targeted for inspections and other enforcement actions. When it chooses these targets, OECA should analyze patterns that have generated Title VI complaints.

- OECA should move rapidly to add enforcement information to EPA's Geographic Information Systems, such as "Windows on My Environment," so that high-risk community residents can learn when nearby facilities are inspected or involved in an enforcement action.

- OECA should strengthen its targeting of enforcement efforts through increased toxics monitoring in disproportionately impacted communities, and should expand the use of funds recovered under Supplemental Environmental Projects for this monitoring.

- EPA program managers should ensure that their permit writers are adequately trained to recognize permit applications involving disproportionate impacts on low-income and people of color communities, be alert to facility applications that may affect these communities, and know how to address these impacts using the agency's legal authorities.

- For permit applications involving issues beyond EPA's jurisdiction, such as noise, traffic, and odor concerns, permitting staff should notify local authorities early and work with local zoning and health agencies on developing solutions for these concerns.

- Regarding permit applications that may affect low-income and people of color communities, EPA permit writers should:

7

- urge permit applicants to discuss their proposals with the affected community as early as possible

- consider whether the affected community has been designated as high priority or high-risk, whether it may be exposed to specific hazardous emissions according to monitoring data, or whether it is burdened by high levels of pollution or significant discharge levels

- take into account community characteristics – such as demographics, language, local institutions, and familiarity with governmental processes – when selecting communication methods and working with the affected public

- choose carefully the arrangements for public meetings – including time, place, meeting room set-up, and agency representatives – to ensure that community members can easily and comfortably participate

- identify ways to mitigate or reduce emissions and other environmental and public health impacts of proposed facilities, such as requiring pollution prevention and implementing environmental management systems

- make full use of all legal requirements and discretionary authorities to consider a community's high risk and disproportionate impacts when developing permit conditions designed to reduce pollution burdens there

- use facilitated dialogues if the suggested decision tree indicates that a neutral third party could produce better results that are acceptable to all parties

- help communities identify technical support and other resources, such as Technical Outreach Services for Communities, that may help them participate more meaningfully during permit negotiations

- give early notice of a permit application to local authorities, especially when there are indications that zoning, health, and other issues may cause community concern about a permit application

Chapter 4

- EPA should consult with state and local health and environmental agencies to address environmental justice concerns and identify high-priority areas where residents are exposed to large amounts of pollution.

- EPA should collect monitoring data from high-risk areas, and use this information as a tool for identifying potential health hazards and helping permit writers to develop appropriate terms and conditions for permits that will address environmental justice concerns. Where monitoring is not practical due to cost or other factors, modeling should be used to estimate impacts on high-priority areas, understanding that modeling is less precise than monitoring. Upon scientific peer review, EPA should utilize the National-Scale Air Toxics Assessment as a screening tool to identify potential high-priority areas where the agency will conduct a thorough examination of pollution sources.

- EPA should evaluate tools that have been developed by its regional and program offices, as well as by the Offices of Policy, Civil Rights, and Environmental Justice. From these evaluations, the agency should identify potential best practices to recommend when developing practical guidance documents about how permitting staffs can incorporate environmental justice into EPA permits nationwide. EPA's Science Advisory Board should review the most useful tools, once they are available, to ensure that the agency's approaches apply good science.

- EPA should work to ensure the accuracy of data on emissions and exposures in specific communities. The accuracy of all data, especially point-source location data for facilities, is critical given that the agency uses this information to analyze very localized pollution impacts, typically the primary concern of high-risk communities.

Chapter 5

- EPA should expand its Technical Assistance Grants and Technical Outreach Services for Communities programs to offer more timely and accessible technical assistance to communities that need this support. This help would allow communities to participate effectively in EPA's air, water, and Resource Conservation and Recovery Act permitting processes, and in efforts to mitigate environmental risks in high-risk communities.

- Using its discretionary authority, EPA should adopt early notice procedures for communities once permit applications are complete, providing the name of an agency community liaison and soliciting community comments prior to negotiating the permit terms and conditions. EPA should expand these efforts beyond an experimental stage and should make them standard operating procedure.

- EPA should use community liaisons in some high-priority communities to assess how such an approach could improve communications and relationships with those communities.

- EPA should expand its public involvement training and offer significantly more training opportunities so that managers, permit writers, and other staff can develop stronger skills in outreach and public involvement techniques. This training is especially important for those who interact with, or make decisions about, the public.

- EPA's public participation resources, including staff training and technical assistance funding, should be expanded to provide greater balance in the amount of EPA support made available for assisting community groups and regulated businesses.

- EPA should use its facilitation and mediation experiences to create, publish, and widely disseminate a decision tree to help EPA staff decide when and under what circumstances dispute resolution and dialogue tools may be useful when dealing with environmental justice concerns. The agency also should make funding available in each region for the sole purpose of providing community and EPA access to facilitation/mediation resources. The decision tree can indicate when such approaches might be helpful in resolving permit controversies.

- EPA should continue to encourage regulated facilities and permit applicants to work with affected communities early in the permitting process, including publishing case studies that demonstrate the value of community involvement, offering outreach training as part of business assistance programs, and other techniques.

- EPA should use various mechanisms to provide information to communities about permit applications, such as more prominent newspaper notices; notices posted in local institutions including libraries, schools, and churches; establishment of a community liaison person; and web-based information. Also, EPA should expand its efforts to provide information in other languages as appropriate, and in easily understandable formats.

ENDNOTES

[1] Office of Environmental Justice, U.S. Environmental Protection Agency, *Guidance to Assessing and Addressing Allegations of Environmental Injustice, Working Draft* (January 10, 2001) 7.

[2] National Academy of Public Administration. *Environment.gov: Transforming Environmental Protection for the 21st Century* November 2000; Washington, DC (November 2000); *Evaluating Environmental Progress: How EPA and the States Can Improve the Quality of Enforcement and Compliance Information* Washington, DC (2001).

[3] Christine Todd Whitman to Assistant Administrators, *et al*, memorandum, *EPA's Commitment to Environmental Justice* (August 9, 2001).

CHAPTER ONE

INTRODUCTION

Congress has passed significant environmental laws over the past 30 years, and EPA and state environmental agencies have implemented them by establishing elaborate permit application and review procedures, including opportunities for public comments. These are designed so that regulatory officials can make informed decisions about whether to allow the emission of specified amounts of pollution that facilities propose. For many years, however, those permitting decisions have failed to account fully for the potential adverse environmental and health impacts on neighborhoods, many of which have already been disproportionately exposed to environmental harms and risks by facility emissions. These highly impacted neighborhoods frequently are home to low-income and people of color residents. These areas are often called "environmental justice communities," but this report uses the terms "disproportionately impacted" or "high-risk" communities to refer to them.

Disproportionately impacted communities have not participated fully or effectively in EPA and state decision-making processes for issuing new facility permits or renewals. Their residents have lacked this capacity because they have had inadequate opportunity for early involvement and little access to direct technical assistance, an important element given the highly complex nature of permitting issues. Consequently, many urban or rural facilities have obtained operating permits while residents in these areas have been less able to voice opposition, monitor the facilities' compliance with conditions of their permits, or take action if emissions exceed allowable levels.

In June 2001, EPA's Office of Environmental Justice asked the Academy to study the agency's programs for issuing air, water, and waste permits. The project's goal is to determine how environmental justice could be incorporated into EPA's permitting programs. The study is also designed to contribute to the office's five-point strategy for integrating environmental justice concerns into the permitting process. The five steps include seeking advice and recommendations on the issue, securing legal and administrative analyses, developing training, ensuring implementation, and assessing results.

This Academy study is intended to help the public better understand how EPA can incorporate environmental justice concerns into its permitting programs under existing legal authorities contained in the Clean Air Act, the Clean Water Act, and the Resource Conservation and Recovery Act. The study has evaluated the agency's efforts to address environmental justice through its permits and has examined ways that EPA can strengthen this effort through improved accountability, community-wide risk reduction efforts, and public outreach.

The Academy Panel and project team have used as their starting point an EPA legal opinion dated December 1, 2000, which concluded that numerous statutes and regulations confer authorities upon the agency to address environmental justice issues within the context of air, water, and waste permits. This study has explored how EPA can incorporate environmental justice concerns into the daily activities of its permitting programs. In addition to these statutes and regulations, the agency has very clear responsibilities under Title VI of the Civil Rights Act of 1964.[1] Moreover, the Council on Environmental Quality (CEQ), which is responsible for federal compliance with the National Environmental Policy Act and the 1994 Executive Order on environmental justice, issued guidance in 1997 to ensure that environmental justice concerns are appropriately identified and addressed "in every recommendation or report on proposals for legislation and other major Federal actions significantly affecting the quality of the human environment."[2] Although EPA may not be required to prepare environmental impact statements for most permits that it issues, CEQ's guidance is instructive in this instance; it establishes an expectation that agency actions will consider environmental justice and that agencies will take steps, such as improved public participation and mitigation of environmental impacts, to address environmental justice issues.[3]

EPA asked the Academy to focus specifically on its direct permitting responsibilities; at the same time, it recognized that state and local agencies issue most permits through their delegated programs. In Fiscal Year 2000, EPA directly issued only 47 air permits – or 1% – of a total of approximately 3,400 permits under the New Source Review, Part 71, and Title V programs. Furthermore, that year EPA issued approximately 4% of the National Pollution Discharge and Elimination System water permits for major and minor individual sources, primarily in states that have not sought EPA's approval for issuance. EPA issued only two of the total 100 waste permits in Fiscal Year 2000.

Nonetheless, it is important to examine the extent to which EPA has incorporated environmental justice into its permitting programs, and how it has done so. These efforts are a valuable indicator of whether the agency has integrated environmental justice into its core mission and key operations. As EPA has encouraged states and the regulated community to address environmental justice concerns in their own permitting programs, it should be a model for demonstrating how this effort can succeed. In fact, states are required to operate their federally delegated programs in a manner that is "at least equivalent to the requirements established by federal law."[4] Recognizing the states' important role in permitting for air, water, and waste programs, EPA's Office of Environmental Justice has asked the Academy to conduct an additional study examining several states' approaches to incorporating environmental justice into their programs.

The Academy Panel evaluated how environmental justice has been incorporated into EPA's permitting programs and considered prior Academy studies of EPA that recommended performance-based management as a way to produce results for achieving the agency's core mission to improve environmental quality.[5] In addition to this study, these Academy studies have stressed the need for EPA to establish clear accountability for results and use appropriate public administration techniques to ensure that its managers and staff are receptive to, and willing to execute fully, its responsibilities in this important area. Reducing pollution burdens on the public is the heart of environmental justice concerns, and EPA's permitting programs can address these problems. At the same time, implementing performance-based management

14

is vital to protecting public health and the environment. Thus, EPA's environmental justice efforts can and should be integrated into all of its programs and its core mission.

A seven-member Panel of Academy Fellows has guided this study. The Panel has provided important oversight and guidance for the project and has formulated its findings and recommendations based on the extensive research conducted by a project team over a five-month period. The research entailed collecting and reviewing available literature on the legal, administrative, and practical aspects of environmental justice and related fields. The project team also conducted extensive interviews with EPA officials and permitting staffs in six program offices at EPA headquarters and five regional offices, as well as with nine state environmental agencies, community and environmental justice group representatives, and regulated industry managers. During its meetings, the Panel received presentations from community groups, state officials, senior EPA managers, industry representatives, academics, and civil rights and environmental lawyers.

For the purposes of this study, the Academy relied upon EPA's definition of environmental justice:

> Environmental Justice is the fair treatment and meaningful involvement of all people regardless of race, color, national origin, culture, education, or income with respect to the development, implementation, and enforcement of environmental laws, regulations, and policies. *Fair treatment* means that no group of people, including racial, ethnic, or socioeconomic groups, should bear a disproportionate share of the negative consequences resulting from industrial, municipal, and commercial operations or the execution of federal, state, local, and tribal environmental programs and policies. *Meaningful involvement* means that: (1) potentially affected community residents have an appropriate opportunity to participate in decisions about a proposed activity that will affect their environment and/or health; (2) the public's contribution can influence the regulatory agency's decision; (3) the concerns of all participants involved will be considered in the decision-making process; and (4) the decision-makers seek out and facilitate the involvement of those potentially affected.[6]

This report is organized in five chapters. Chapter Two examines the role of EPA's leadership and top managers in ensuring that the principles of environmental justice are actually embedded within the agency's day-to-day operations. Chapter Three describes EPA's current air, water, and waste permitting programs, identifies opportunities for inclusion of environmental justice concerns, and suggests tools and techniques for implementation. Chapter Four places environmental justice in the context of EPA's mission and overall program responsibilities. It also identifies existing tools and approaches for addressing environmental justice concerns in a proactive manner. Chapter Five examines EPA's mandates and opportunities for public participation in the permitting process, the barriers and issues arising from the environmental justice context, and the strategies and approaches to address issues of concern.

ENDNOTES

[1] Title VI, Civil Rights Act of 1964, U.S.C. 42, Sec 2000d *et seq.*

[2] Council on Environmental Quality, *Environmental Justice Guidance Under the National Environmental Policy Act* (December 10, 1997), 7-8.

[3] Ibid.

[4] National Academy of Public Administration, *Environment.gov: Transforming Environmental Protection for the 21st Century,* (2000), 12.75.

[5] National Academy of Public Administration (the Academy), *Environment.gov: Transforming Environmental Protection for the 21ˢᵗ Century, Research Papers 11-17, Volume III,* (2000); the Academy, *Resolving the Paradox of Environmental Protection: An Agenda for Congress, EPA, & The States* (1997); and the Academy, *Setting Priorities, Getting Results: A New Direction For EPA* (1995).

[6] U.S. EPA, Office of Environmental Justice, *Guidance to Assessing and Addressing Allegations of Environmental Injustice: Working Draft* (January 10, 2001), 7.

CHAPTER TWO

LEADING CHANGE AT EPA: STRONG LEADERSHIP CAN PRODUCE RESULTS

FINDINGS

Finding 1: EPA's leadership has articulated a clear commitment to environmental justice that predates the 1994 Executive Order and continues into the current administration.

Finding 2: Despite the commitment of senior EPA leadership, environmental justice has not yet been integrated fully into the agency's core mission or its staff functions. Expectations for specific outcomes have not accompanied these commitments, nor has the agency adopted methods for measuring progress in achieving them or accountability to ensure that EPA managers and staff work toward implementing environmental justice policies.

Finding 3: EPA has significant statutory and regulatory authority, as well as numerous opportunities for exercising discretion, to incorporate environmental justice considerations into its air, water, and waste permitting programs.

Finding 4: The existing agency culture is one barrier to incorporating environmental justice into EPA's permitting programs. This culture does not treat environmental justice as a central element of the agency's core programs.

INTRODUCTION

President Clinton's Executive Order 12898 on environmental justice,[1] as well as policy statements by Administrator Christine Todd Whitman[2] and former EPA Administrators Carol M. Browner[3] and William K. Reilly,[4] have clearly articulated to agency staff the importance of achieving environmental justice. Top-level EPA regional managers have also emphasized environmental justice issues. This senior-level support, however, has not yet consistently translated into changes in how many program managers and regional staff, including permit writers, conduct their daily work.

There may be many reasons why this has not occurred, including inadequate tools and training, workload burdens, and a lack of understanding among most EPA staff that environmental justice is vital to their activities. One senior EPA official noted that it must be made clear to all staff that environmental justice is integral to EPA's core mission; the fact that environmental justice problems still exist demonstrates that EPA has not succeeded in addressing environmental issues as well as it might have otherwise.

Overall, the primary reason this translation has not occurred is because top EPA managers have not established clearly expected outcomes for addressing environmental justice. Nor have they measured the progress of their programs in achieving these outcomes, or held other managers and staff accountable for producing reasonable progress. Although the agency has initiated many environmental justice activities over the last decade, it still has not integrated environmental justice into fundamental agency operations, including permitting.

To ensure that environmental justice becomes embedded in EPA's core programs, functions, and culture, the agency requires:

- clearer risk reduction goals for disproportionately impacted communities
- consistent and sustained leadership attention at every level, to ensure the agency's progress in meeting these goals and to incorporate environmental justice considerations into daily EPA activities
- appropriate program accountability measures to achieve desired outcomes
- practical tools that staff can use when responding to environmental justice concerns
- training for staff that will allow them to gain a fuller understanding of environmental justice issues, appreciate the direct relationship to EPA's mission, and acquire skills for working more effectively with the public
- adequate time and resources so staff can carry out their responsibilities for protecting public health, including addressing environmental justice concerns
- rewards and performance evaluation mechanisms that recognize the importance of this work and the staff who make special efforts to promote these goals

BACKGROUND

Over the past decade, EPA has demonstrated a commitment to achieving environmental justice through a number of actions, such as:

- adopting environmental justice as one of its seven guiding principles
- issuing clear policy statements that require staff to integrate environmental justice into every EPA program, policy, and activity
- developing and staffing agency offices to support implementation of environmental justice goals
- providing financial support for community-based projects
- engaging visible support among political and career managers for environmental justice

Current EPA leadership strengthened this commitment when Administrator Christine Todd Whitman issued an August 9, 2001 memorandum that reaffirmed the agency's determination to promote environmental justice. She required EPA staff to incorporate environmental justice considerations into their policies, programs, and activities, including both memoranda of agreement between air, water, and waste programs and EPA's regional offices, and National Environmental Performance Partnership Agreements with the states.

EPA's work on environmental justice issues began with a 1990 meeting of the Congressional Black Caucus, academics, social scientists, and political activists. The parties shared information and concerns about EPA's inconsistent enforcement and inspections, allowing excessive environmental risks in minority and low-income communities. EPA leadership responded by establishing the Environmental Equity Workgroup shortly thereafter, and it issued a 1992 report entitled *Reducing Risks in All Communities.*[5] The report validated concerns raised at earlier meetings and found that people of color communities and low-income neighborhoods were often exposed to greater environmental pollution and public health risks than the general population. Based on this finding, the workgroup recommended that EPA adopt a nationwide policy on environmental justice and that it establish an office within EPA to ensure that the policy would be integrated into normal EPA operations. The Office of Environmental Equity, established in November 1992, was renamed the Office of Environmental Justice (OEJ) two years later. In 1994, EPA created the National Environmental Justice Advisory Council (NEJAC) to provide advice and recommendations to the Administrator on environmental justice matters and their integration into EPA's core programs; measurement and evaluation of progress; existing and future data systems assessment, technologies, and data collection; and education, training, and outreach activities. [6]

In 1995, EPA issued its first environmental justice strategy to implement President Clinton's Executive Order.[7] The strategy required the agency to develop a plan to incorporate environmental justice into the core aspects of every EPA program, policy, and activity. To implement the strategy, a network of environmental justice coordinators at the headquarters and regional levels was created, and special groups were established to provide oversight of how environmental justice was implemented by air, water, and waste program staff. For instance, the Office of Enforcement and Compliance Assurance (OECA) established an Environmental Justice Coordinating Council to ensure that environmental justice became an integral part of its operations;[8] and the Office of Solid Waste and Emergency Response (OSWER) developed a strategic plan to guide its efforts.[9]

Moreover, EPA began to offer technical and financial support to communities to address their environmental justice concerns.[10] In 1994, OEJ inaugurated the Environmental Justice Small Grants Program. For the past eight years, grants totaling over $12 million have been provided to more than 900 recipients that have implemented community-based projects to remedy environmental justice problems and to promote education and outreach on avoiding or reducing environmental hazards in specific neighborhoods.[11]

In 1996, NEJAC's Enforcement Subcommittee asked how EPA had integrated environmental justice considerations into its permits. It determined that unexplored opportunities existed for EPA to apply its authorities for environmental justice issues for permitting decisions.[12] That same year, the subcommittee developed a recommendation that EPA use its existing authorities to respond to environmental justice concerns in its permitting actions.[13] In 1999, NEJAC held a three-day meeting that produced a report entitled *Environmental Justice in the Permitting Process.*[14] The report principally recommended that the Administrator should:

- clarify EPA's legal authority to deny, condition, or require additional procedures for a permit on environmental justice grounds
- provide leadership to create a better understanding of cumulative impacts, degree and disproportionality of risk, and community demographics and how they might relate to the permit process

- strengthen and highlight public participation requirements in the permitting process
- ensure the equitable enforcement of federal laws
- provide guidance to state, regional, local, and tribal governments on the environmental justice implications of facility siting and local zoning ordinances for permitting decisions[15]

On December 1, 2000, EPA's General Counsel issued a legal opinion that analyzed agency authorities under current air, water, and waste statutes. It found that many programs can appropriately incorporate environmental justice concerns in their permits.[16] In addition, EPA's statutory authorities for air, water, and waste contain similar provisions for addressing environmental justice procedurally through various public participation requirements.[17]

GENERAL COUNSEL CONCLUSIONS

The General Counsel's opinion found that environmental justice authorities in EPA's water statutes and regulations focus on reducing water pollution from industrial sources and preventing the possible health effects from eating contaminated fish. Many Clean Water Act provisions address these concerns, including water quality standards, National Pollutant Discharge Elimination System (NPDES) permits, and Section 404 permits for dredging and filling, as do the Safe Drinking Water Act and the Marine Protection, Research, and Sanctuaries Act. Specific authorities available to EPA include approving or disapproving state water quality standards, adopting conditions for NPDES permits, and denying permits if underground injection of fluids may endanger public health.

Regarding waste disposal, the Resource Conservation and Recovery Act (RCRA) authorizes EPA to condition or even deny permits "if EPA determines that operation of the facility would pose an unacceptable risk to human health and the environment and that there are not additional permit terms or conditions that would address such risk."[18] The agency has interpreted this provision to include consideration of "cumulative risks due to exposure from pollution sources in addition to the applicant facility; unique exposure pathways and scenarios (e.g., subsistence fishers, ... etc.); [or] sensitive populations (e.g., children with levels of lead in their blood, individuals with poor diets)."[19] RCRA also allows EPA to address environmental justice concerns when processing permits for hazardous waste treatment, storage, and disposal facilities, including incinerators and landfills. EPA may apply conditions to RCRA permits that incorporate environmental justice concerns, such as requirements for reasonable monitoring, minimum buffer zones from sensitive areas – including schools and residential neighborhoods – and, in the case of land disposal permits, health assessments. RCRA further authorizes EPA to consider such factors as cumulative risks, unique exposure pathways, and sensitive populations when establishing permitting or clean-up priorities.[20]

EPA has numerous authorities under the Clean Air Act to consider environmental justice when issuing various air permits. For example, under the New Source Review program, a permit applicant in an area that has not attained air quality standards must perform an analysis of "alternative sites, sizes, production processes, and environmental control techniques."[21] The agency must then consider the possible benefits of the proposed source, and whether the environmental and social costs imposed on the community would outweigh them if the permit is approved. The NSR program appears to be unique in allowing EPA to grant permits only if applicants can demonstrate, through evaluation of the environmental effects on a community, that a facility's benefits outweigh the costs. EPA's Environmental Appeals Board has affirmed the agency's authority to consider environmental justice for air permits.[22] EPA's other air permitting programs generally require consideration of environmental justice issues, but these primarily involve procedural requirements for public comment and review of proposed permits.

ACCOUNTABILITY MECHANISMS AND MEASURES OF PROGRESS FOR ADDRESSING ENVIRONMENTAL JUSTICE

Following issuance of its environmental justice strategic plan in 1995, EPA adopted environmental justice as one of its guiding principles,[23] attempting to make it an element of all agency programs and decisions. EPA's strategy includes five major elements: [24]

1. public participation, accountability, partnerships, outreach, and communication with stakeholders
2. research on public health and environmental impacts
3. data collection, analysis, and stakeholder access to public information
4. protecting Native Americans and other indigenous groups
5. enforcement, compliance assurance, and regulatory reviews

Nonetheless, EPA has not established performance, outcome, or accountability measures for these five elements, making it extremely difficult to determine whether the agency has made any progress in implementing its strategy. Although EPA committed to issuing biennial reports on environmental justice activities, the most current report was prepared in 1998. Thus the agency lacks an ongoing record of accomplishments and a current listing of its recent activities to address environmental justice. Moreover, the last report only documented EPA activities, not their relevance to desired outcomes.

Academy research indicates that EPA has not established clear mechanisms for holding its managers and staff accountable for implementing the agency's environmental justice strategy. Instead, it shows that performance for programs of particular interest and concern to the environmental justice community – like air, water, and waste permitting – has not been tracked or evaluated to determine if or how EPA staff has integrated these concerns into EPA activities. This lack of accountability creates many problems and sends a message to managers and staff that the agency does not really place a high priority on environmental justice issues. One interviewee stated that EPA staff would pay attention to environmental justice if their managers expected them to focus on these issues. Other interviewees enumerated the reasons why they did not consider environmental justice in their programs. At the end of the interview session, they confirmed that there might be opportunities in their programs to address these concerns, creating greater inclusiveness in their public participation efforts at a minimum.

EPA ACTIVITIES ADDRESSING ENVIRONMENTAL JUSTICE ISSUES

Despite the lack of accountability mechanisms and performance measures, EPA has undertaken numerous environmental justice activities. It has addressed these concerns in various ways, generally and specifically for air, water, and waste permits. The Office of Solid Waste and Emergency Response (OSWER) launched several important projects that implement specific requirements of EPA's 1995 environmental justice strategy and the office's own strategic plan, which incorporates environmental justice into its public participation procedures for siting and permitting hazardous waste facilities. OSWER's permitting-related initiatives include:

- a policy directive from OSWER's Assistant Administrator requiring that all office policies, guidance, and regulations be reviewed for environmental justice considerations[25]
- publishing *Social Aspects of Siting a Hazardous Waste Facility,*[26] which encourages facility managers to consider the potential impact on nearby communities when they evaluate various locations for new or expanded operations
- issuing *Waste Transfer: Involved Citizens Make a Difference*[27] to explain how citizens can influence regulatory decisions about waste facilities
- distributing *Public Involvement in Environmental Permits: A Reference Guide,*[28] which provides guidance to regulators and others on how the public can be more effectively involved in the permitting process for waste facilities, for air, and for water permitting decisions.

OSWER has provided technical assistance to communities through several mechanisms and has trained EPA staff on more effective ways to involve community groups in program decisions, including its annual community involvement conference on public participation best practices.[29]

EPA's waste program made an initial $50,000 investment to the Technical Outreach Services to Communities program.[30] This contribution was intended to help residents of high-risk communities gain access to technical experts who can advise on specific waste facilities and potential permit conditions. The solid waste program also has developed a community outreach toolkit and extensive public participation guidance for its permit writers and other staff.[31] In addition, the office has established an annual employee award process to recognize staff who have conducted special effective public outreach. Through its innovative approaches to public participation, the office has gained the reputation as a leader in public participation and addressing environmental justice concerns.

The Office of Air and Radiation also has undertaken specific activities to address permit-related environmental justice concerns. It sponsored national programs like Title V permit training for citizen groups that is provided in each EPA region, and citizen training on urban air toxics and improving the capacity of urban communities to reduce exposure to air toxics.[32] The office also offers scholarships to community group members so they can participate in training opportunities. One community source interviewed gave high marks to the Title V training, both for its content and for the air office's involvement with community people during the course design.

In addition, the air office has conducted special outreach and communications for high-risk communities under the Tier II/Gasoline Sulfur Rule and permitting.[33] It has incorporated environmental justice criteria in its *Improving Air Quality with Economic Incentive Programs* guidance document[34] for air emissions trading. Environmental justice criteria also have been included in its urban air toxics strategy, and pilot programs have begun to test methodologies for reducing overall toxic burdens in urban communities. One such program was initiated in Puerto Rico as part of its Pollution Prevention and Permitting Program (P4) (See Textbox, *P4 Permit for Merk Pharmaceuticals*). The air office has developed a best practices guide for reducing air emissions from waste transfer stations. Working with the waste and water offices, it also spearheaded the development of a draft guidance document on toxics reduction, providing a compendium of techniques and strategies for reducing toxic loadings in local areas, a particular concern to environmental justice communities.

P4 PERMIT FOR MERCK PHARMACEUTICALS

EPA's Office of Air and Radiation (OAR) has issued a number of innovative, flexible air permits as part of its Pollution, Prevention and Permitting Program (P4). The main tools used in P4 permitting include advance approvals for predetermined changes to be made at a facility under a Title V operating permit, as well as the use of cap permits and plant-wide applicability limits (PALs).

A good example of how flexible permits work is the P4 permit that Region II developed for Merck Pharmaceuticals, in cooperation with the Puerto Rico Environmental Quality Board (EQB). EPA used a plantwide applicability limit, coupled with advanced approvals, to provide Merck with the flexibility and streamlined administrative requirements it needed to respond quickly to market demands.

Additionally, Merck committed to report regularly to the community about its pollution prevention activities and to provide additional recordkeeping, reporting, and emissions data. EPA, Puerto Rico EQB, and Merck held meetings with local community groups (several meetings were conducted in Spanish) and industry to explain the innovative features of the permit and how it reflected the total air emissions associated with the facility. Puerto Rico EQB provided financial resources for the community to hire its own consultant to review and explain the permit to local groups.

The flexibility associated with the P4 process allowed the community to obtain a better picture of facility-wide operations and to receive more comprehensive emissions data for the Merck facility. Overall, the community was assured that the total air emissions associated with the Merck facility would not increase above the levels provided in the P4 permit without further public participation opportunities.

Upon completion of the public comment period, local community representatives did not file adverse comments about the public participation or innovative features associated with the Merck permit.

Source: U.S. EPA, Region II Air Program.

The Office of Water sponsored a 1998 meeting with environmental justice stakeholders to address issues arising from the implementation of the Safe Drinking Water Act. Eleven cities participated in the meeting via video conferencing, and they suggested that the office make greater efforts to reach minority communities and to provide understandable information to the public on a more timely basis. Also, the office issued EPA's first federal Fish Consumption Advisory in 1997,[35] an especially important document for subsistence communities that have low-income, Native American, and/or people of color residents, who depend upon fish as a major source of protein in their diets. However, Academy research for this study did not elicit any permit-related efforts by the water office to address environmental justice concerns.

EPA regions and program offices have taken other important steps that are directly related to the environmental justice issues arising from permitting. These include regional development of policies, guidance documents, training, and tools to address disproportionate impact and public participation issues of concern to environmental justice communities. EPA regions have crafted various local Geographic Information System (GIS) tools to incorporate data, such as information on emissions and emission sources, demographics, housing, and health conditions, for use in environmental justice assessments. The Office of Environmental Justice (OEJ) also has developed *The Environmental Justice Query Mapper*, as part of a joint project with the Office of Environmental Information.[36] The Mapper is the only agency-centered, Internet-based GIS for evaluating environmental justice issues. The office now co-chairs a national project designed to create a uniform, national approach for using GIS to conduct environmental justice assessments.[37]

OEJ also has developed a national environmental justice training program, a workshop on the Fundamentals of Environmental Justice. This workshop was designed in collaboration with EPA staff; other federal, state, and tribal agencies; community, labor, and faith-based organizations; industry; and academia. It provides historical background on environmental justice, analytic tools, and examples of how this issue can be integrated into EPA programs. The program will train 3,000 people from EPA, states, tribes, communities, and industry during the next year.[38]

Other EPA offices have significantly contributed to addressing environmental justice issues associated with permitting, such as research on cumulative impact assessment and advice on more effective public participation. The Office of Research and Development has sponsored workshops to clarify community-assessment needs and identify the tools needed to address them, as part of the office's effort to use science to address critical agency concerns. The Office of Policy, Economics, and Innovation has developed a community-specific study to test a method for assessing cumulative exposures at the community level and to gain a better understanding of how such assessments can be done in such a site-specific way. The office recently developed EPA's new *Public Involvement Policy*,[39] which provides information on how EPA can conduct outreach about environmental justice concerns. This policy is designed to produce a robust yet consistent approach to public participation across the agency. The innovation office has also developed *Guidelines for Preparing Economic Analyses.*[40] These guidelines explain how EPA can analyze the economic impacts of its program regulations and policies, and how it can assess costs and benefits among various segments of the population, focused especially on disadvantaged and vulnerable groups.

The EPA activities described above are intended to be illustrative, not exhaustive. Although EPA has conducted significant activities to incorporate environmental justice concerns into its air, water, and waste permits, Academy research shows that the agency has not fully integrated these concerns into its day-to-day operations.

CLOSING THE LOOP ON IMPLEMENTING ENVIRONMENTAL JUSTICE

The issues identified in EPA's 1995 environmental justice strategy remain as relevant today as they were when the strategy as created.[41] For instance, there is widespread consensus that more effective and timely public involvement in the permitting process is critical to ensure that the agency identifies and addresses environmental justice concerns. The 1995 strategy called for EPA to guarantee active citizen involvement in its programs by utilizing participation models such as the one developed by the NEJAC, offering training for citizens, and publishing public notices in languages other than English, when possible and appropriate. Interim performance measures also could be established for the percentage of permits in which citizens are given early notice of permit applications. Similar performance measures could be established for every other area identified in the 1995 strategy.

Academy research revealed the difficulties in determining what EPA offices have done to implement the 1995 strategy. The agency's *1998 Environmental Justice Biennial Report: Moving Towards Collaborative and Constructive Problem-Solving*[42] is the most current compilation of EPA's environmental justice activities, yet it is more than three years old. The activities of various regions and offices are listed in that report's chapter on public participation, outreach, and training. The entries do not, however, explain whether these initiatives have been integrated into such core program functions as permitting, or whether EPA's environmental justice objectives have been achieved as a result of these activities. Academy research suggests that EPA is not yet able to demonstrate how or whether its environmental justice projects are producing the intended outcomes for achieving environmental justice issues. Attempts to gather more information on the results of these efforts have been made even more difficult because EPA programs do not normally keep basic and coherent information about their environmental justice activities, either at office or agency-wide levels.

CHANGING EPA'S CULTURE TO INCORPORATE ENVIRONMENTAL JUSTICE CONCERNS

Several of those interviewed for this study identified the change-resistance of EPA's culture as a significant obstacle to incorporating environmental justice into the agency's routine activities, including permitting. Culture change requires a demonstrated commitment to environmental justice at every level of EPA leadership. Several interviewees reported that one major agency program has no interest in working on these issues.

To ensure real culture change, staff at all agency levels must understand that environmental justice embodies every major element of EPA's core mission. Indeed, environmental justice concerns encompass citizens' rights to equal environmental protection, communities' right-to-know, informed public participation, risk reduction, protecting the most susceptible populations, and reducing cumulative exposure. Connecting these issues with EPA's core mission is an important undertaking that should be a high priority among EPA's leadership and management. One senior manager stated that it is a challenge to help all EPA employees perceive environmental justice as part of their jobs. This manager pointed out that this change is difficult because the concept of environmental justice is ambiguous to many people.

To change EPA's culture, agency employees must clearly understand and respect the fact that residents of disproportionately impacted communities frequently possess valuable information that EPA needs to make well-informed decisions. Thus, communities can help the agency build effective solutions. One community activist noted that her community's relationship with EPA changed when EPA staff "learned to listen." Agency appreciation that community participation adds value can produce institutional changes, improving the flow of important information between EPA and the community.

EPA's waste office is the agency leader in public participation, in part because it has chosen to exceed its minimum regulatory requirements and to provide more effective public input and involvement through numerous techniques. This strategy has been driven by program needs and top-level commitment to ensuring that staffs offer meaningful public involvement supported by the requisite resources.

Leadership is critical to changing EPA's culture by demonstrating the importance of environmental justice. That can be accomplished by establishing clear expectations and insisting that agency managers and employees not treat environmental justice as an optional exercise. Setting expectations includes making policy decisions, such as those needed for guidance on how environmental justice will be treated in the context of EPA's permitting programs, that make the agency's commitment operational day-to-day. It also means setting consistent, uniformly applied expectations, allowing reasonable flexibility for program differences, and providing additional time for employees to learn how to incorporate these issues into their daily work. For instance, the agency can allow for some variation in approaches to public participation for air, water, and waste permits, yet still expect permit writers in those programs to demonstrate that they are considering environmental justice issues.

EPA also can facilitate culture change by making it easier for its employees to incorporate environmental justice into their day-to-day activities. Interviewees stated repeatedly that EPA staff have a real need for tools and guidance documents that are practical and sensitive to workload realities for staff who are on the agency's front line for implementing environmental justice, such as permit writers. Encouraging creativity and flexibility can help EPA employees to address important issues like environmental justice, even within workload constraints. Identifying every possible efficiency, however, still may not address the very real need for employees to have adequate time for doing this work.

Evaluating EPA employees on whether they produce positive results for environmental justice can be an important way of motivating the agency's program offices, regions, and individual employees to remain focused on meeting these goals. Evaluations aimed at producing specific results should be combined with a system of rewards that recognizes managers and staff who make special efforts to address environmental justice concerns through permits and who reach out to communities before making agency decisions. One EPA office found that awards are an important incentive for staff to give environmental justice issues appropriate attention.

RECOMMENDATIONS

- Building on Administrator Whitman's recent environmental justice memorandum, the Assistant Administrators for Air, Water, and Waste, and the Regional Administrators should reinforce the importance of this policy, its role in implementing EPA's core mission, and the expectation that their managers and staff will implement environmental justice in their projects and activities.

- EPA should finalize its draft national environmental justice guidance and develop practical tools for permit writers to identify and address environmental justice issues arising in air, water, and waste permits.

- The Offices of Air, Water, and Waste should develop strategic plans demonstrating how environmental justice will be integrated into the substance and procedures of their permitting programs, and they should carefully examine how they can use the authorities set forth in the General Counsel's legal opinion dated December 1, 2001, to incorporate environmental justice concerns into permits for new and ongoing projects.

- Each office's plan for incorporating environmental justice in its permitting programs should include goals, measures of performance, expected outcomes, accountability mechanisms, and time frames for meeting the goals.

- EPA should establish an accountability process that includes clear performance measures for evaluating how well employees – both managers and staff – are able to incorporate environmental justice into air, water, and waste permits.

- EPA should identify disproportionately impacted and other adversely affected communities and establish explicit goals for reducing risks there. The agency should set clear expectations for producing results that are directly linked to the agency's mission and give staff an important performance measure that they can support in a whole-hearted fashion. These tasks could also provide measures of EPA's progress in implementing environmental justice and could be reinforced by agency-wide reporting that tracks their progress.

- EPA should develop a communication mechanism for sharing information with all air, water and waste programs, regional offices, and states about effective tools for addressing environmental justice, including descriptions of best practices and lessons learned. This mechanism should coordinate EPA's activities for incorporating environmental justice into permitting, so that permit writers in all the air, water, and waste programs and regional offices can become more effective and gain greater efficiency and effectiveness in responding to environmental justice concerns.

- EPA should evaluate the effectiveness of its national workshop on the Fundamentals of Environmental Justice to determine how well it meets its intended objectives, including the effective implementation of environmental justice in permitting.

- EPA should develop a program for rewarding employees' extra efforts to address environmental justice in permitting, through recognition in existing national awards and development of headquarters and regional office recognition programs.

ENDNOTES

[1] Executive Order 12898, *Federal Actions to Address Environmental Justice in Minority Populations and Low Income Populations* (1994).

[2] Christine Todd Whitman to Assistant Administrators, *et al,* memorandum, *EPA's Commitment to Environmental Justice* (August 9, 200).

[3] Carol M. Browner, *EPA's Environmental Justice Strategy* (April 3, 1995).

[4] U.S. EPA, "Environmental Equity: EPA's Position, Protection Should Applied Fairly," *EPA Journal* (March/April 1992): 18-22.

[5] U.S. EPA, Office of Policy Planning and Evaluation, *Environmental Equity: Reducing Risk for All Communities, Vol. I and II*, EPA A230-R-92-008A (June 1992).

[6] National Environmental Justice Council Charter (July 29,1999).
Available at http://es.epa.gov/oeca/main/ej/nejac/charter.html.

[7] U.S. EPA. Office of Environmental Justice, Environmental Justice Strategy: Executive Order 12898 (April 1995).

[8] U.S. EPA, *Environmental Protection Agency Environmental Justice 1994 Annual Report.*

[9] U.S. EPA, *Environmental Justice Homepage.* Available at http://www.epa.gov/swerosps/ej/index.html#ejhist

[10] U.S. EPA, Office of Enforcement and Compliance Assurance, *Small Grants Program Application Guidance FY 2000* (October 2001).

[11] U.S. EPA, Office of Environmental Justice, *Environmental Justice Small Grants Program: Emerging Tools for Local Problem-Solving* (1999).

[12] Richard Lazarus, "Integrating Environmental Justice Into Environmental Permitting Decisions," Presentation before the Environmental Justice Panel of the National Academy of Public Administration (June 14, 2001).

[13] Ibid.

[14] National Environmental Justice Advisory Council, *Environmental Justice in The Permitting Process: A Report from the National Environmental Justice Advisory Council's Public Meeting on Environmental Permitting— Arlington, Virginia November 30-December 2, 1999*, EPA/300-R-00-004 (July 2000).

[15] National Environmental Justice Advisory Council, letter to Carol M. Browner, *Environmental Justice in the Permitting Process*, (August 3, 2000).

[16] Gary S. Guzy to Steven A. Herman, *et al*, memorandum, *EPA Statutory and Regulatory Authorities under Which Environmental Justice Issues May Be Addressed in Permitting* (December 1, 2000).

[17] Ibid.

[18] Ibid., 3.

[19] Ibid., 3.

[20] Ibid., 3.

[21] Ibid., 11.

[22] In re: Knauf Fiber Glass, GmbH, PSD Appeal Nos. 99-8 through 99-72, Environmental Appeals Board, Decided March 14, 2000.

[23] Browner, Carol M., *EPA's Environmental Justice Strategy* (April 3, 1995).

[24] Ibid.

[25] Elliott P. Laws to Director, Office of Emergency and Remedial Response, *et al*, memorandum, *Integration of Environmental Justice Into OSWER Policy, Guidance, and Regulatory Development* (September 21, 1994).

[26] U.S. EPA, Office of Solid Waste and Emergency Response, *Social Aspects of Siting RCRA Hazardous Waste Facilities*, EPA530-K-00-005 (April 2000).

[27] U.S. EPA, Office of Solid Waste and Emergency Response, *Waste Transfer Stations: Involved Citizens Make the Difference*, EPA530-K-01-003 (January 2001).

[28] U.S. EPA Office of Solid Waste and Emergency Response, *Public Involvement in Environmental Permits: A Reference Guide*, EPA-500-R-00-007 (August 2000).

[29] U.S. EPA Office of Solid Waste and Emergency Response, *OSW Environmental Justice Program Strategy*. Available at http://www.epa.gov/osw/ej/.

[30] Suzanne Wells and Pat Carey, U.S. EPA, Office of Solid Waste and Emergency Response, Interview (September 10, 2001).

[31] Ibid.

[32] U.S. EPA, Office of Air Quality Planning and Standards, Technology and Transfer Network, *The National Training workshop on Local Urban Air Toxics Assessment and Reduction Strategies*. Available at http://www.epa.gov/ttn/atw/wks/mainwks.html.

[33] Anna Wood, U.S. EPA, Personal Correspondence (November 7, 2001).

[34] U.S. EPA, Office of Air and Radiation, *Improving Air Quality with Economic Incentive Programs*, EPA-452/R-01-001 (January 2001).

[35] U.S. EPA, Office of Enforcement and Compliance Assurance, *1998 Environmental Justice Biennial Report: Moving Towards Collaborative and Constructive Problem-Solving*, EPA 300/R-00-004, (July 2000) 4.7.

[36] U.S. EPA, Office of Enforcement and Compliance Assistance, *Environmental Justice Query Mapper* (2001). Available at http://es.epa.gov/oeca/main/ej/ejmapper/.

[37] Barry E. Hill, U.S. EPA, Office of Environmental Justice, Personal Communication (November 13, 2001).

[38] Nicholas Targ, U.S. EPA, Office of Environmental Justice, Interview (November 13, 2001).

[39] U.S. EPA, Office of Policy Economics and Innovation, *Work Related to Environmental Justice (2000-2001)* (October 31, 2001).

[40] Ibid.

[41] Carol M. Browner, *EPA's Environmental Justice Strategy* (April 3, 1995).

[42] U.S. EPA, *1998 Environmental Justice Biennial Report* (July 2000).

CHAPTER THREE

PRACTICAL TOOLS FOR PERMIT WRITERS TO ADDRESS
ENVIRONMENTAL JUSTICE CONCERNS

FINDINGS

Finding 5: A recent General Counsel's legal opinion makes it clear that the Clean Air Act, Clean Water Act, and Resource Recovery and Conservation Act provide ample authority for EPA's permitting staff to address high-risk community concerns when developing the terms and conditions of individual facility permits. EPA Administrator Christine Todd Whitman has reaffirmed this opinion in her August 9, 2001 memorandum to senior EPA officials.[1]

Finding 6: EPA managers have not routinely provided straightforward, practical tools and procedures to their permitting staff for incorporating community concerns into permits, nor have they directed the staff to ensure that environmental justice concerns are systematically considered in EPA's permitting programs.

Finding 7: Many EPA permit writers have not had an opportunity to learn how they can contribute to resolving environmental justice concerns by obtaining more information about the community that may be affected by a proposed permit; the nature of the risks that the community faces; community concerns related to the proposed facility; the community's capacity to participate in the permitting process; and the best methods for communicating with the community.

Finding 8: Given that its legal authority to issue permits for particular facilities is based on the Clean Air Act, Clean Water Act and Resource Recovery and Conservation Act, EPA has limited ability to deal with other common concerns in high-risk communities, such as noise, traffic, and odor.

Finding 9: EPA's credibility relating to permitting programs in high-risk communities depends upon timely and rigorous review of permit renewals for existing facilities and on using opportunities to enforce visibly their permit conditions, including increased inspections and local monitoring of environmental conditions.

BACKGROUND

Although specifics may vary, the basic procedures for EPA's air, water, and waste permitting programs are the same. The process begins when a company chooses to build or modify a facility and determines that an environmental permit is required. The company then prepares a permit application and submits it to the appropriate EPA regional office. The region's air, water, or waste permitting staff review the application and determine whether the applicant has provided the necessary information; staff may request additional details if information is lacking. Once the application is complete, EPA's permit writers technically review the proposal, develop permit conditions designed to ensure compliance with applicable environmental standards and requirements, and establish the monitoring and reporting requirements. It is not uncommon for the technical review to entail interaction between the applicant and permitting staff. Once a draft permit is complete, EPA publishes a public notice and announces a formal public comment period, normally 30 days long. Following the comment period, the permit writers review the public comments, make appropriate adjustments in the permit terms and conditions, and forward the application for the agency's final decision (See Figure 3-1).

Various opportunities abound throughout the permitting process for more timely and meaningful interaction between the agency and the affected community. For example, the applicant could work voluntarily with the community even before submitting the draft application; this would provide the applicant a clearer understanding of public concerns and the opportunity to resolve them. Also, permitting staff could give the affected community and local governments early notice when a permit application is received and later when the application is complete. The community, local governments, and the permit applicant could discuss or negotiate the application before it reaches the draft permit stage. When differences of opinion or difficult issues arise, the permit writers could use facilitated dialogues to help the parties develop a consensus on permit terms and conditions, rather than rely solely on the formal public comment period.

EPA's experience with dispute resolution approaches including facilitated dialogues and more formal mediation, together with a review of the available literature, should provide the agency with a rich set of information about when these tools are most useful and how to structure these dialogues (timing, location, facilitation, identifying the appropriate stakeholders) to maximize the likelihood of success. This kind of information could be extremely useful to permit staff and managers if embodied in a decision tree, which would aid in determining when dialogue techniques would be most appropriate. National distribution of information on public involvement tools, already proven to be successful, in conjunction with the decision tree would provide permitting staff with important information needed to shape efficient and effective public participation. EPA's Region II provides a good example of how this process can work in practice.

Region II has direct permitting responsibilities for programs in Puerto Rico, and it processed sixty water permits and five air permits for prevention of significant deterioration since the Executive Order on environmental justice was issued in 1994. The region has prepared extensive evaluations to identify and address possible issues related to environmental justice for five of its air permits and six of its water permits.[2] In performing this analysis, the region's permit writers have relied on the region's recent policy statement that sets forth their responsibilities for implementing environmental justice.[3] The policy is founded on some basic principles that include "early and meaningful" involvement of the affected community.[4]

Region II also has provided its permit writers with practical tools, including a methodology for determining areas that can be identified as "communities of concerns" and a GIS, which generates maps showing the demographics for areas with high numbers of low income and people of color residents, as well as the site-specific environmental burdens of those communities. As a result, the region has had positive experiences in addressing environmental justice concerns through the permitting process. Its staff has learned additional lessons for improving this process. Those improvements include:

1. earlier and more frequent community interactions
2. public availability sessions to discuss concerns prior to the final permit
3. greater understanding about how to mesh permitting legal requirements with environmental justice concerns
4. consideration of cumulative impacts, even when potential emission levels are below certified levels requiring cumulative impact studies
5. translation of materials for non-English speaking communities

Region II acknowledges that its process for reviewing permits and involving the public is more complex and time consuming than the routine permitting procedures.[5] This is partly attributable to its desire to address environmental justice concerns. Nevertheless and more importantly, the region has learned that these complexities should not prevent EPA from addressing environmental justice concerns through its permitting programs; it can do so consistent with its responsibilities under the 1994 Executive Order. Additionally, the region has provided technical assistance to its states and copies of its GIS-based demographic screening tool to states, permit applicants, and others, to encourage the identification and addressing of environmental justice concerns in the permitting process[6] (See Textbox, *Region II*).

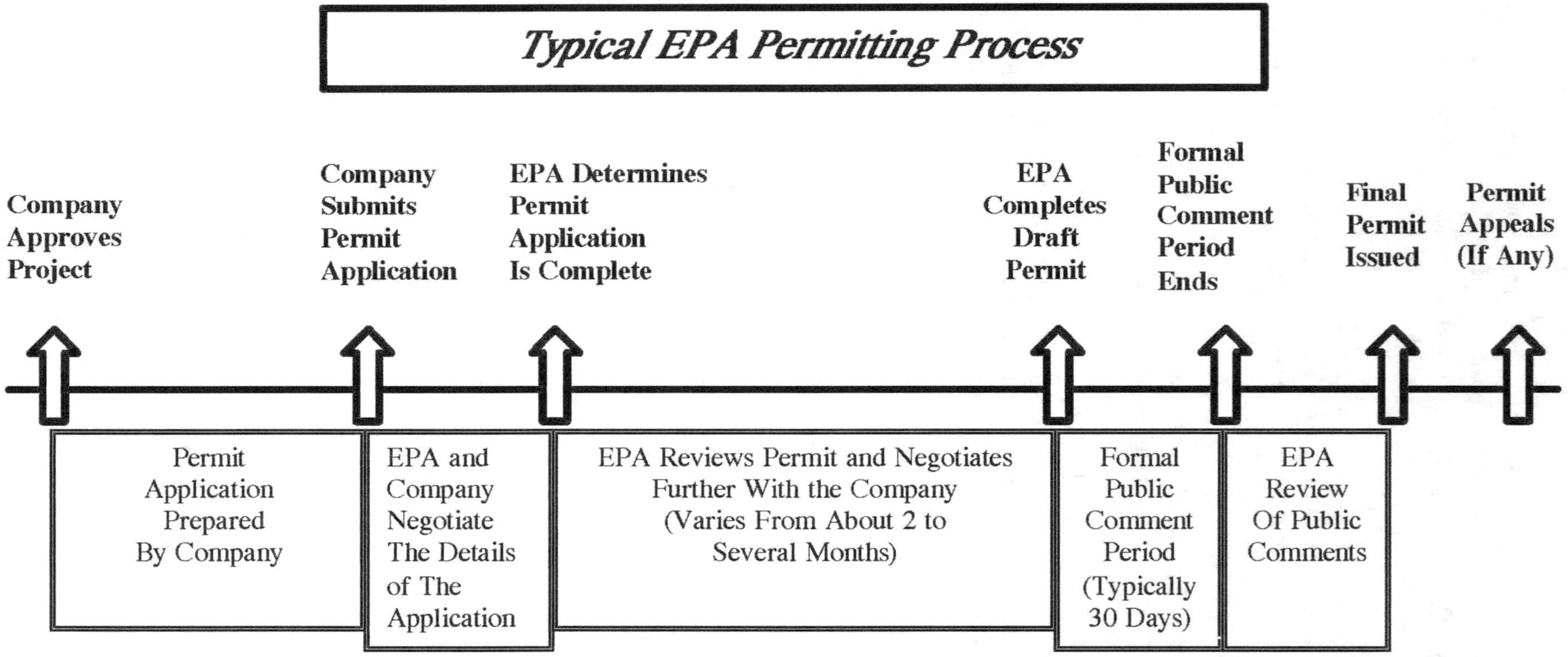

Typical EPA Permitting Process

Company Approves Project

Company Submits Permit Application

EPA Determines Permit Application Is Complete

EPA Completes Draft Permit

Formal Public Comment Period Ends

Final Permit Issued

Permit Appeals (If Any)

Permit Application Prepared By Company

EPA and Company Negotiate The Details of The Application

EPA Reviews Permit and Negotiates Further With the Company (Varies From About 2 to Several Months)

Formal Public Comment Period (Typically 30 Days)

EPA Review Of Public Comments

Figure 3.1

36

REGION II

EPA's Region II has taken extra steps to incorporate environmental justice concerns. It has created an Interim Environmental Justice Policy that emphasizes meaningful and early public involvement, early identification of permit applications that may raise environmental justice concerns, community identification of environmental justice issues, and responses to allegations of disproportionate impacts. Region II also has developed an accountability segment in its plans to evaluate how well they are addressing and resolving environmental justice problems.

The Interim report pays particular attention to the following categories:

- **Ways to identify cases with Environmental Justice Issues**.

  Key areas of focus include:

  ✓ Setting up geographic boundaries for communities
  ✓ Making comparisons between the demographics for a community of concern and demographics from statistical reference data
  ✓ Development of comprehensive Environmental Load Profiles. This profile is based on salient characteristics that serve as indicators of environmental burden and provide consistent basis for comparisons. Region II's environmental Burden Indicators include the following components: Toxics Release Inventory Air Emissions, Facility Density/Population Density, Land Use Index, and Ambient Air Quality Mapping (Attainment/Non-Attainment Designation).

- **Addressing disproportionate impacts and responding to concerns.**

  Region II has observed that:

  ✓ Enhancing public participation helps to promote environmental justice by ensuring that citizens' concerns and information about the affected community have been factored into the EPA's decision-making process.
  ✓ Using authority to set permit conditions gives the EPA the discretion to take disproportionate effects into account when developing permit conditions on monitoring levels, risk reduction and prevention, and preparedness for accidental releases.
  ✓ Encouraging voluntary Stakeholder Agreements for mitigating community impacts from a facility; stakeholder involvement increases the ability to reach "good neighbor" agreements that are advantageous to all who are involved.

Source: U.S. EPA, Region II, *Interim Environmental Justice Policy* (December 2000).

AUTHORITIES FOR INDIVIDUAL PERMITS

A December 2000 General Counsel's legal opinion explained the scope of EPA's legal authorities for addressing environmental justice concerns when issuing individual permits. The opinion described those actions that are "legally permissible" under the General Counsel's interpretation of the agency's primary authorizing statutes. Although these interpretations are legally permissible, the General Counsel noted that the actions needed to implement this authority may not "be uniformly practical or feasible given policy or resource considerations" and recognized that there may be "important considerations of legal risk that would need to be evaluated."[7] This opinion, combined with Administrator Whitman's 2001 memorandum,[8] provides the legal authority and management directive for EPA's program offices to begin to utilize additional opportunities for integrating environmental justice issues when preparing EPA permits, developing new rules, issuing emission standards, and preparing new guidance documents.

Several individuals interviewed for this study suggested that new permitting approaches designed to address environmental justice issues must be "simple" and "doable." EPA program managers can make significant progress in addressing these concerns by using their legal authorities to address disproportionate impacts; exercising their discretionary authority for earlier and more frequent public participation; and translating these authorities into practical steps that can be used for air, water, and waste programs. A permitting checklist developed by Washington State's Department of Ecology (see Appendix A) provides a practical, straightforward approach that permit writers can use when determining whether a specific permit may raise environmental justice issues. Only recently implemented, this checklist will likely trigger additional analysis in communities where permit writers identify possible environmental justice concerns, and help to reinforce the importance of environmental justice in the permitting staff's day-to-day work.

The time needed to focus on environmental justice issues and work with communities is another key issue for permitting staff. One project manager responsible for EPA permits in Indian country reported that permit applications raising environmental justice issues often require much more interaction between EPA staff and affected parties.[9] However, EPA models for determining its permit writers' appropriate workloads do not account for the additional time and effort needed in these situations.[10] Nonetheless, it is clear that additional time is needed for enhanced public involvement in the permitting process.

Texas' environmental agency has revised its permitting procedures to comply with a new state law that requires public notice of a permit upon an application's completion,[11] rather than when agency staff and the applicant have finished negotiation on a draft permit. The agency's public meetings increased from about 25 prior to the early notice procedure to 89 in the first year that the new law took effect. Similarly, Texas received comments on more than 15 percent of total applications in 2000, compared with 10 percent in 1999. In addition, the states' permit writers spend significantly more time interacting with community members than they did before the new procedures were adopted.[12]

Agency leadership and the Academy Panel both view environmental justice as part of EPA's core mission. Consequently, it is incumbent on agency staff to find ways that they can resolve environmental justice concerns, especially once EPA has provided staff with training and information on these issues. For example, permit writers can pay greater attention to the nature of the community affected by a proposed facility, the risks and concerns for its residents, its ability – or lack thereof – to become involved in reviewing the permit, the technical and legal resources available within and outside EPA to help its members understand the context for a facility and participate in permit negotiations, and the best ways for the agency to communicate with it. Regional staff interviewed believed that new methods for public involvement are key to EPA developing a more effective and acceptable permitting process and resolving permit disputes.

Community groups not only are focused on a permit's terms and conditions, but they also frequently seek to ensure that a facility actually complies with those conditions.[13] More visible EPA enforcement and regular facility inspections in these communities can help to provide this assurance.[14] Once a permit is issued, EPA's vigilance is important to establish credibility for the permitting process and to demonstrate that the agency has meaningfully incorporated environmental justice concerns into that process.[15] EPA could devote greater inspection and enforcement resources toward monitoring facility performance in high-risk communities, thus increasing EPA's presence. Additional monitoring of facility emissions and ambient conditions in affected communities, as well as public reporting of those monitoring results, also would facilitate EPA enforcement, encourage facilities to maintain compliance, and allow community groups to track environmental conditions in their neighborhoods. Increased public access to emissions information and EPA enforcement results can help citizens to determine whether nearby facilities are abiding by their permit requirements.

EPA could strengthen the credibility of permit conditions by placing additional monitors in high-risk communities – such as mobile monitoring equipment that can address site-specific problems – and using monitoring data to develop conditions for new, revised, or renewed permits. In several instances, EPA has used supplemental enforcement projects (SEPs) to fund additional community monitoring;[16] these commonly offset a portion of an administrative or civil penalty that would otherwise be levied against a regulated facility during an enforcement action. SEPs are designed to return a benefit, or mitigate some of the damage, to a community affected by the facility's pollution.[17] Thus, SEPs are well suited to address environmental justice issues.

Finally, EPA must eliminate backlogs of expired permits and permit renewals, to mitigate the potential for facilities to operate under outdated or potentially less protective permit conditions.[18]

RECOMMENDATIONS

- In the short-term, EPA should determine whether it can provide communities with earlier notice of permit applications, at least as soon as agency staff determine the applications to be complete. This would provide more opportunities for the public to interact directly with the agency's permit writers and allow consideration of community information and concerns during the drafting and negotiation stages.

- In the long-term, EPA should revise its permitting regulations to ensure that nearby communities are notified of a permit application as early as possible, and certainly as soon as the application is complete.

- EPA should revise its public notification practices to ensure that notices are provided in languages common to affected communities and placed at libraries, churches, community centers, and other locations where many community residents can see them.

- EPA managers should provide their permit writers with checklists or similar tools, to aid them in identifying and considering potential environmental justice concerns.

- EPA budget and administrative staff should recognize the additional time and effort that permit writers need to develop permit conditions for environmental justice issues and to work more closely with community groups. They should adjust the agency's workload models as appropriate to determine the average number of permits that each writer is expected to handle.

- EPA's air, water, and waste programs should ensure that their permits fully implement current environmental standards and should modify or add standards, if necessary, to ensure that pollution levels are reduced to better protect public health.

- EPA's air, water, and waste programs should place high priority on the elimination of permit renewal backlogs to ensure that facilities have conditions that are as up-to-date and protective as possible, especially for those affecting high-risk or disproportionately impacted communities.

- EPA's air, water, and waste programs should develop specific guidance documents on the legal requirements and discretionary authorities that permit writers have to require additional monitoring and public reporting in disproportionately impacted communities.

- EPA should consider using facilitated dialogues as part of its permitting process, at least in some cases, by creating and utilizing a decision tree approach. This approach could help to incorporate environmental justice concerns in EPA permits by: (1) preparing permit conditions that address community concerns; (2) facilitating interactions between permit applicants and affected residents; (3) providing an opportunity for local authorities to address such issues as noise, odor, and traffic that EPA cannot resolve; and (4) crafting voluntary agreements among permit applicants, the community, EPA, and relevant state or local agencies.

- EPA's Office of Enforcement and Compliance Assurance (OECA) should use environmental justice as a criterion for deciding the locations and types of facilities targeted for inspections and other enforcement actions. When it chooses these targets, OECA should analyze patterns that have generated Title VI complaints.

- OECA should move rapidly to add enforcement information to EPA's GIS, such as "Windows on My Environment," so that high-risk community residents can learn when nearby facilities are inspected or involved in an enforcement action.

- OECA should strengthen its targeting of enforcement efforts through increased toxics monitoring in disproportionately impacted communities, and should expand the use of funds recovered under Supplemental Environmental Projects for this monitoring.

- EPA program managers should ensure that their permit writers are adequately trained to recognize permit applications involving disproportionate impacts on low-income and people of color communities, be alert to facility applications that may affect these communities, and know how to address these impacts using the agency's legal authorities.

- For permit applications involving issues beyond EPA's jurisdiction, such as noise, traffic, and odor concerns, permitting staff should notify local authorities early and work with local zoning and health agencies on developing solutions for these concerns.

- Regarding permit applications that may affect low-income and people of color communities, EPA permit writers should:

  - urge permit applicants to discuss their proposals with the affected community as early as possible

  - consider whether the affected community has been designated as high priority or high-risk; whether it may be exposed to specific hazardous emissions according to monitoring data; or whether it is burdened by high levels of pollution or significant discharge levels

  - take into account community characteristics – such as demographics, language, local institutions, and familiarity with governmental processes – when selecting communication methods and working with the affected public

- choose carefully the arrangements for public meetings – including time, place, meeting room set-up, and agency representatives – to ensure that community members can easily and comfortably participate

- identify ways to mitigate or reduce emissions and other environmental and public health impacts of proposed facilities, such as requiring pollution prevention and implementing environmental management systems

- make full use of all legal requirements and discretionary authorities to consider a community's high risk and disproportionate impacts when developing permit conditions designed to reduce pollution burdens there

- use facilitated dialogues if the suggested decision tree indicates that a neutral third party could produce better results that are acceptable to all parties

- help communities identify technical support and other resources, such as Technical Outreach Services for Communities, that may help them participate more meaningfully during permit negotiations

- give early notice of a permit application to local authorities, especially when there are indications that zoning, health, and other issues may cause community concern about a permit application

ENDNOTES

[1] Christine Todd Whitman to Assistant Administrators, *et al,* memorandum, *EPA's Commitment to Environmental Justice* (August 9, 200).

[2] Terry Wesley and other Region II Staff Interviews (October 11, 2001).

[3] U.S. Environmental Protection Agency, Region II, Interim Environmental Justice Policy (December 2000).

[4] Ibid.

[5] Interviews with Region II staff.

[6] Terry Wesley, Personal Correspondence, November 26, 2001.

[7] U.S. Environmental Protection Agency, Office of General Counsel, memorandum, *EPA Statutory Authorities Under Which Environmental Justice Issues May Be Addressed in Permitting* (December 1, 2000) 1.

[8] Christine Todd Whitman to Assistant Administrators, *et al,* memorandum, *EPA's Commitment to Environmental Justice* (August 9, 200).

[9] Karen Scheuermann, Region IX, Interview (September 4, 2001).

[10] Ibid.

[11] Texas Health and Safety Code, as amended, section 382.056 (1999).

[12] Texas Natural Resources Conservation Commission staff, Interviews (September 25, 2001).

[13] Albertha Hastens, Louisiana Environmental Action Network; Joan Mulhern, Earthjustice; and Damon Whitehead, National Black Environmental Justice Network, Interviews (September 18 and October 23, 2001).

[14] Mary M. O'Lone, Lawyers' Committee for Civil Rights Under Law, Remarks before the National Academy of Public Administration (August 30, 2001).

[15] Ibid.

[16] Region IV staff, Interviews (September 24, 2001).

[17] U.S. Environmental Protection Agency, Office of Compliance Assurance and Enforcement, *Final Supplemental Enforcement Projects Policy* (May 1, 1998).

[18] Malcolm Woolf and Apple Chapman, Office of General Counsel, Interviews (August 23, 2001).

CHAPTER FOUR

PERMITTING AS AN ELEMENT OF EPA'S STRATEGY TO PREVENT POLLUTION AND REDUCE RISK

FINDINGS

Finding 10: EPA does not now have a routine process for identifying high-risk communities and giving them priority attention to prevent pollution and reduce existing public health hazards.

Finding 11: Many parties support the need for EPA to conduct cumulative risk assessments when evaluating permit applications, but the current state of this science has not advanced sufficiently to conduct these assessments. However, EPA has efforts underway to improve the science so that it will be more feasible and practical. While waiting for cumulative risk assessment science to advance, EPA, several states, and citizen groups have developed and applied other tools that analyze exposures of disproportionately impacted communities to actual or potential amounts of multiple pollutants. More frequent and comprehensive environmental monitoring in these communities can help EPA to determine whether they need priority attention.

Finding 12: Limited environmental data, and their lack of accuracy, are barriers to risk reduction, particularly when analyzing very localized, community-level environmental conditions and impacts.

Finding 13: Absent a consistent, national approach for assessing risks, several EPA regional offices have developed tools for evaluating disproportionate impacts from pollution. These tools, combined with EPA regional experiences, have created an important body of practical experience. Yet, EPA has not evaluated or catalogued them so that the agency's permitting programs can learn about best practices, the elements needed to develop a national guidance document on analyzing cumulative risks, or any potential concerns about the scientific validity of the tools.

BACKGROUND

The Need to Evaluate Cumulative Risks

Identifying high-risk communities is an important first step that will enable EPA to set goals and focus attention on reducing environmental hazards there. For several years, EPA has acknowledged the need to develop scientifically valid methods for assessing cumulative risks created by pollution, which in turn create high-risk situations. This need also was noted by the National Research Council in *Science and Judgment in Risk Assessment*[1], and by the Presidential/Congressional Commission on Risk Assessment and Risk Management in *Assessment and Risk Management in Regulatory Decision Making.*[2]

Practical considerations have driven EPA's agenda in this area, as well. These include Congress' approval of the Food Quality Protection Act of 1996,[3] which requires, among other things, that EPA analyze cumulative effects of chemical exposures occurring concurrently, rather than perform single chemical assessments. Complaints filed under Title VI of the 1964 Civil Rights Act,[4] which can require EPA to assess potential cumulative risks in high-risk communities, have created additional pressure to develop these tools. EPA's Title VI Advisory Committee report, *Next Steps for EPA, State, and Local Environmental Justice Programs*, recommended that the agency significantly expand its efforts "to research the nature and existence of cumulative exposures and synergistic effects and the risks they pose."[5] In addition, some states have officially recognized the need for cumulative risk assessment. For example, Texas' state legislature recently required its environmental agency to develop an approach for evaluating cumulative environmental and public health impacts.[6]

Efforts to Evaluate Cumulative Exposures

Recognizing a growing internal and external consensus, EPA's Science Policy Council issued a 1997 guidance document on planning and scoping for cumulative risk assessments.[7] The memorandum accompanying that document noted the latter's potential for evaluating the exposures of particular segments of the population. The Council intended that the guidance would help EPA to be "better able in many cases to analyze risk by considering any unique impacts the risks may elicit due to the gender, ethnicity, geographic origin, or age of the affected population."[8] The memorandum further stated that "where data are available. . . [EPA] may be able to determine more precisely whether environmental threats pose a greater risk" to specific groups or populations.[9] However, the memorandum noted that the guidance did not consider "the social, economic, behavioral, or psychological factors that also may contribute to adverse health effects. These include, among others, such factors as existing health conditions, anxiety, nutritional status, crime, and congestion."[10] The Council omitted these problems from its guidance due to the lack of data, yet high-risk communities have raised some of these issues, like health conditions, as critical concerns. Although the GIS Mapper and Stressed Community Concept prepared by EPA's Region III[11] have attempted to capture the broader spectrum of health and social data, only the Mapper has been tested and neither tool has undergone scientific peer review for reliability and, as a practical matter, they remain a future prospect.

The Council's guidance and other assessments use a very broad definition of cumulative impact assessment. Nonetheless, this term is frequently used to describe several distinct types of analysis, including:

- **additive impacts:** exposure to the same chemical from multiple sources
- **aggregate effects:** exposure to more than one chemical with the same health effect or end point
- **cumulative risk**: exposure to multiple chemicals that may originate from several sources and have different impacts or end points, and the interactions of these chemicals with one another (synergistic or antagonistic effects)

Other EPA efforts to evaluate how multiple sources may affect public health include the draft cumulative risk assessment guidelines developed by the Office of Pesticide Programs for implementing the Food Quality Protection Act,[12] and the National-Scale Air Toxics Assessment for characterizing the potential health risks associated with inhaling 33 high-priority air pollutants.[13] In addition, the Cumulative Exposure Project, housed in EPA's Office of Policy, Economics, and Innovation, has prepared a case study on community-specific cumulative risk assessment.[14] The project worked with members of a mostly minority community and nearby permitted facilities to gain a better understanding of the practicalities involved when performing assessments. EPA has also initiated research projects to examine cumulative and synergistic effects created by urban air toxics, and it has helped states to assess cumulative risk when establishing total maximum daily loads under the Clean Water Act.[15]

EPA is developing a framework on how to conduct a cumulative risk assessment. The agency's Science Policy Council has taken steps to identify the basic elements of the cumulative risk assessment process.[16] This framework will be reviewed by EPA's Science Advisory Board and will be presented to the Science Policy Council for review and approval. Upon completion, EPA plans to develop a guidance document on conducting cumulative risk assessments.

CURRENT EPA TOOLS AND APPROACHES TO REDUCE RISK

Cumulative impacts are key to high-risk community concerns. These communities are concerned about the impacts of individual chemicals, as well as the health hazards created by cumulative exposures from multiple sources and chemicals. Although EPA has made progress in developing an approach for conducting cumulative risk assessments, it does not have practical tools for doing so, especially in the relatively brief time frame required for reviewing permit applications. More practical tools for conducting cumulative risk assessments may be available in the future, but less complex methods of assessing risks are needed now. The 1998 report of EPA's Science Advisory Board, *Review of Disproportionate Impact Methodologies,*[17] recommended that EPA use simpler methodologies to identify chemicals or their classification that may be of concern prior to performing more detailed risk assessments. In this regard, Academy research identified several methods that EPA could utilize in the short term for analyzing the multiple exposures that are typical in high-risk communities. At the same time, these tools are less complex than cumulative risk assessment.

Monitoring Exposures

Ambient monitoring of existing pollution levels is one currently available method for EPA to evaluate the additive impacts and aggregate effects of community exposure. Monitoring results could aid EPA's permit writers in understanding a community's actual exposures to chemicals with similar effects. In one EPA region, for instance, scientists have determined that one or two chemicals are responsible for 90 to 95 percent of the environmental risks in 80 to 85 percent of the census blocks for one study area.[18] If enhanced monitoring identifies high-risk chemical emissions and potential health impacts among residents with additive or aggregate exposures, permit writers would have support for crafting conditions in new permits or renewals, thereby reducing emissions in high-risk communities.

Identifying higher risk communities based on emissions from multiple sources would enable EPA to devise strategies involving enforceable and voluntary components, both of which would be designed to improve the environment. These provisions might include pollution prevention to reduce high-risk chemicals, closer scrutiny of new and renewal permit applications, and voluntary pollution reduction agreements involving communities, regulated industries, and EPA. These approaches are consistent with the EPA strategic plan's fourth goal, which is to prevent pollution and reduce risk in communities, homes, workplaces, and ecosystems.[19]

EPA is reassessing its ambient monitoring network and hopes to redesign it.[20] Such an effort would offer an important opportunity for incorporating environmental justice concerns into the agency's overall effort to gain a better understanding of cumulative and residual risks. Provided that the redesigned monitoring network would cover high-risk communities with environmental justice concerns, EPA could ensure the availability of information needed by permit writers to address cumulative impacts.

Many recognize monitoring as an important tool for identifying and solving environmental problems. For example, EPA's Region VI has reached agreement with industry sources and with the states' support to invest $1.2 million for an improved monitoring network, responding to environmental justice concerns raised in local communities.[21] The parties collectively agreed that they will address problems identified by monitoring and that community residents will receive monitoring results so they can help determine any needed corrective action. The parties believe that improved monitoring will allow them to resolve environmental justice issues and fully inform communities about potential problems and the outcomes of their joint problem-solving efforts (See Textbox, *Monitoring and Cleanup Initiative for Calcasieu Estuary*).

MONITORING AND CLEANUP INITIATIVE FOR THE CALCASIEU ESTUARY

The Louisiana Department of Environmental Quality (LADEQ) is coordinating an initiative to measure the ambient air quality in the Lake Charles/Calcasieu Parish area with support from the Lake Area Industry Alliance (LAIA), EPA, and local communities. The initiative will significantly enhance the existing ambient air-monitoring program being conducted by LADEQ. The intent of the initiative is to measure the levels of volatile organic compounds (VOCs) and dioxins that are present in the area. The results will provide additional information on air quality in Southwest Louisiana and insight into what additional steps LADEQ and EPA must take to protect the health and safety of area residents.

The Calcasieu Estuary includes the Calcasieu River from northern Moss Lake to the salt-water barrier at Lake Charles. The estuary is an industrialized area where several petrochemical and agrochemical plants manufacture and process diverse products such as petroleum, sodium hydroxide, chlorine, Teflon, butadiene, synthetic rubber, trichloroethylene, and perchloroetheylene.

In March 1999, EPA decided to conduct a federal Remedial Investigation and Feasibility Study to evaluate sediments in the Calcasieu Estuary. The principal pollutants in the area are:

- PCBs
- hexachlorobenzene
- hexachlorobutadiene
- mercury
- zinc
- ethylene dichloride
- lead
- copper

In cooperation with the local governments and area industries – Conoco, PPG, and Olin – EPA is also responding to the community's concerns about fish advisories and dioxin exposures, as well as industry issues of cost and corporate responsibility for cleaning up the sediments.

For more information, see http://www.epa.gov/earth1r6/6sf/sfsites/sitedesc.htm and http://www.deq.state.la.us/evaluation/calcasieu/

A lack of adequate resources and qualified staff can be a barrier to establishing an improved monitoring network. Yet EPA should treat environmental justice concerns as an indicator of the need to analyze public exposures and deploy monitors to sensitive areas. These locations include places where there are community complaints or where EPA has identified "hot spots." These places should be given high priority for allocation of the agency's scarce monitoring resources so they can be used to address real environmental and human health concerns. The agency should then ensure that its permitting staff uses best practices and creativity to solve these problems more effectively. For instance, EPA could deploy mobile monitoring stations, like the ones housed in two EPA regions to service the agency, to measure excessive amounts of air pollution in high-risk communities.

Cost is a critical factor when utilizing such sophisticated equipment as the mobile monitors housed in Regions II and VI. However, EPA should consider assessing he utility of less costly alternatives, including the mobile air-monitoring laboratory developed in Jacksonville, Florida. The Jacksonville project, recognized by the Environmental Law Institute in *Fresh Air: Innovative State and Local Programs for Improving Air Quality* as an innovative approach to improving air quality, is a significantly less expensive version of EPA's mobile unit.[22] These mobile monitoring stations may have great value in identifying high-priority areas where EPA should pursue comprehensive follow-up monitoring and assessment of community exposures.

Modeling Exposures

Comparing monitoring to modeling, one interviewee stated that monitoring results show higher pollution levels than models for the same area; this would suggest inadequacies with modeling. Yet, despite its advantages, monitoring may not always be feasible. In some situations, modeling may be a legitimate means of identifying potential high-priority environmental problems in high-risk communities. Pilot-tested models, such as one that compared monitoring and modeling results for the same Texas community,[23] may offer EPA promising alternatives to monitoring. The Texas project is part of Region VI's effort to develop a tool for examining additive risks when the same air pollutant is released from several sources in a given community.

EPA's National-Scale Air Toxics Assessment (NATA) offers yet another method for utilizing modeling data to identify potential areas of concern that need further, closer evaluation[24] (See Textbox, *National Air Toxics Assessment*). For air toxics, at a minimum, NATA will assist EPA in targeting its limited resources to reduce pollution in high-risk areas and address environmental justice concerns. Academy research did not uncover similar modeling methods for waste or water pollution.

NATIONAL AIR TOXICS ASSESSMENT

Under the Clean Air Act, EPA is required to regulate emissions of 188 air toxics. It is currently conducting a National-Scale Air Toxics Assessment (NATA) of 33 air toxics that present the greatest threat to public health in the largest number of urban areas. This assessment also includes diesel particulate matter, which is used as a surrogate measure for diesel exhaust. NATA includes four steps that use data from 1996:

1. compiling a national emissions inventory of air toxics emissions from outdoor sources

2. estimating ambient concentrations of air toxics across the contiguous United States

3. estimating population exposures across the contiguous United States

4. characterizing potential public health risks due to inhalation of air toxics, including both cancer and noncancer effects

NATA's goal is to identify air toxics that pose the greatest potential concern in terms of contribution to population risk. EPA will use the results to set priorities for the collection of additional air toxics data, such as emissions and ambient monitoring data.

AIR POLLUTANTS INCLUDED IN THE ASSESSMENT	
	18. nickel compounds
2. ethylene oxide	19. chloroform
	20. polychlorinated biphenyls (PCBs)
4. formaldehyde	21. chromium compounds
	22. polycyclic organic matter (POM)*
6. hexachlorobenzene	23. coke oven emissions
	24. quinoline
8. hydrazine	25. dioxins/furans**
	26. 1, 1, 2, 2-tetrachloroethane
10. lead compounds	27. ethylene dibromide
	28. perchloroethylene
12. manganese compounds	29. propylene dichloride
-	30. trichloroethylene
14. mercury compounds	31. 1, 3-dichloropropene
	32. vinyl chloride
16. methylene chloride	33. ethylene dichloride
	34. diesel particulate matter
* also represented as 7-PAH	
** results not yet available	

For more information, see http://www.epa.gov/ttn/atw/nata/34poll

51

Analyzing and Reducing Cumulative Exposures

Permit writers should have the necessary tools to determine whether a proposed facility poses cumulative risks to its host community. They also should have tools to reduce these risks if they find such problems exist. EPA's Office of Air and Radiation, working with the Office of Solid Waste and Emergency Response, the Office of Pollution Prevention and Toxic Substances, and the Office of Water, has developed a guidance document on how to reduce toxic emissions in local areas.[25] Additionally, the air office is conducting a pilot project in Cleveland, Ohio to characterize indoor and ambient toxics and to determine how to reduce them.[26] EPA should record the lessons learned from such initiatives and make them available to the water and waste programs. This can be done through a guidance document for permitting staff that explains how they can resolve problems of cumulative impacts involving the permit applicant and other existing sources in the same community.

Academy research identified several tools and methodologies that guide EPA permitting staff when conducting impact assessments for environmental justice issues. EPA's former Office of Policy developed a methodology for analyzing community-specific cumulative exposures.[27] This report may provide additional insights to EPA offices about more broadly applicable methods for conducting a study of cumulative exposures in a specific community. Region II uses a methodology for creating an "environmental load profile analysis" by finding indicators of the "environmental burden" that a particular community may experience.[28] Meanwhile, Region VI is conducting a pilot study in a Texas community that uses a new approach for analyzing additive risk from several sources of the same pollutant.[29] Upon completion, the region will submit this methodology to EPA's Science Advisory Board for peer review.

When evaluating complaints under Title VI of the Civil Rights Act and preparing its *Draft Revised Guidance for Investigating Title VI Administrative Complaints Challenging Permits*,[30] EPA has compiled more information and experience about how to evaluate cumulative impacts. The agency should draw upon these lessons as it designs more practical, consistent approaches to assessing cumulative impacts when considering permit applications with potential impacts on high-risk communities.

As noted earlier, EPA's former Office of Policy conducted a comprehensive community-specific study that assessed total exposures to more than 100 pollutants across multiple exposure pathways.[31] This study was conducted in a low-income community covering approximately five square miles and containing a high concentration of industrial facilities, waste storage and treatment facilities, garbage transfer stations, and transportation routes that produced significant emissions from mobile sources. The policy office worked with the community, Region II, the state, and other stakeholders to operate this multi-year project, aimed at evaluating cumulative exposures and identifying community characteristics that might be associated with disproportionately high exposure levels. The study also was designed to test "a methodology for community specific cumulative exposure analysis that ... might be useful to other communities."[32]

Reducing Pollution in Specific Communities

Some community groups have viewed cumulative impact assessments and local cumulative impact reductions as important tools in addressing environmental justice concerns. Some of EPA's Title VI Advisory Committee members stated that programs designed to address permitting on the basis of airsheds or watersheds "have the potential to define and ameliorate the cumulative effects of emissions on communities more effectively than individual decisions, although they may present similar scientific and technical challenges."[33] They noted, however, that the value of these programs should not diminish the importance of considering environmental justice implications of individual permits, as these can have significant implications for communities that are over-burdened with pollution.

California's Air Resources Board has taken the area-wide concept to a more local scale, and has considered ways to reduce pollution impacts on a neighborhood level. In conjunction with Region IX, the Department of Housing and Urban Development, the National Institute of Environmental Health Sciences, the San Diego Air Pollution Control District, and the Environmental Health Coalition, the California Air Resources Board is developing guidelines on how to evaluate strategies for reducing air pollution impacts on neighborhoods. This project is called the Neighborhood Assessment Program[34] (See Textbox, *California's Neighborhood Assessments*). Its primary purpose is to develop pollution assessment tools, but it will also include development of risk reduction techniques should the project uncover a high-risk situation in San Diego's Barrio Logan community where the study is being conducted. The Neighborhood Assessment Program builds on a prior study by the South Coast Air Quality Management District, called the Multiple Air Toxics Exposure Study II (MATES II).[35] MATES II was a community-based monitoring, analysis, and modeling project focused on residential areas potentially impacted by nearby sources of toxic emissions. The federal Inter-Agency Work Group on Environmental Justice,[36] coordinated by EPA's Office of Environmental Justice, is currently conducting an evaluation of the Barrio Logan project, using MATES II as a measure.[37]

CALIFORNIA'S NEIGHBORHOOD ASSESSMENTS

The California Air Resources Board (CARB) proposes to use the following work plan to develop guidelines for evaluating strategies for reducing air pollution impacts at the neighborhood level.

Objective: To develop and coordinate the Neighborhood Assessment Program (NAP) within CARB. To investigate whether or not cumulative air pollution impacts differ between neighborhoods within a designated region. To focus on developing guidelines for CARB and other stakeholders to use to evaluate cumulative impacts in a neighborhood.

1. **Program Development**
   (a) Work Group; (b) Evaluate Existing Programs; (c) Program Coordination; (d) Environmental Justice Mission Statement; (e) Communication Plan

2. **Cumulative-Impact Assessment Methodology**
   (a) Identify Data and Methodology Gaps; (b) Develop Dispersion and Impact Assessment Model; (c) Evaluate Methodologies and Protocol; (d) Work Cooperatively with the Office of Environmental Health Hazard Assessment (OEHHA); (e) Peer Review

3. **Barrio Logan Pilot Study**
   (a) Coordination and Risk Communication; (b) Monitoring; (c) Emission Inventory Development; (d) Data Analysis and Impacts Evaluation

4. **Supplemental Neighborhood Monitoring and Impacts Evaluations**
   (a) Develop Neighborhood Assessment Criteria; (b) Neighborhood Identification; (c) Neighborhood Monitoring and Evaluations

5. **Health Evaluation Efforts**
   (a) MATES II Health Correlation; (b) Neighborhood Health Evaluations; (c) Cumulative Impact Indices; (d) Identify Co-funding Sources

6. **Risk Reduction Strategies**
   (a) Near-term Risk Reduction; (b) Regulatory Framework; (c) Long-term Risk Reduction Strategies

7. **Evaluation Guidelines**
   (a) Develop Guidelines; (b) Peer Review and Stakeholder Outreach; (c) Board Action

For more information, see http://www.arb.ca.gov/ch/napworkplan.htm

Community-based efforts to reduce air toxics received the attention of Clean Air Communities (CAC), a nonprofit effort established in 1999 by environmental groups, states, industry, a foundation, and a regional air association. CAC is committed to air pollution reduction strategies in low-income and other communities that are disproportionately affected by air pollution. The Northeast States for Coordinated Air Use Management (NESCAUM)[38] recently inaugurated CAC's first project. NESCAUM has collaborated with EPA, the New York Department of Environmental Conservation, and community-based environmental organizations. In the study community, one in three children has asthma. The project aims to eliminate 2,000 tons of air pollution from diesel exhaust at the South Bronx's Hunts Point Cooperative Market by electrifying trucks and refrigerated trailers while they idle at the market (See Textbox, *Clean Air Communities*).

CLEAN AIR COMMUNITIES

Environmental organizations based in New York and state agencies have received much publicity for developing a strategic plan, called the Clean Air Communities initiative, to address air pollution by installing new clean air technology in low income or people of color communities. With Governor Whitman's support, they have been able to establish innovative public-private partnerships to correct environmental hazards at the local level. New York communities that have been traditionally affected by air pollution are of special interest to these organizations. The intent of their program is to empower communities by implementing locally based energy efficiency and clean air strategies. They intend to promote environmental equity through funding, technical assistance, and implementation of clean air technologies in targeted urban areas. Through the implementation of the Clean Air Community initiative, they have been able to achieve drastic reductions of diesel emissions from idling trucks in a South Bronx neighborhood by developing a truck trailer electrification station.

Source: Clean Air Communities, *New Collaborative Commits $5 Million for Clean Air Projects in New York City's Impacted Communities*, 2000.

Data accuracy and availability are critical to successful problem identification, resolution, and accountability for results. The Academy has noted the importance of accurate data in several prior reports, including *environment.gov* and *Evaluating Environmental Progress: How EPA and the States Can Improve the Quality of Enforcement and Compliance Information.*[39] Academy research indicates that data adequacy and accuracy have specific implications for environmental justice issues because they are very localized. The lack of accurate point-source location data can produce results that do not correctly capture the potential exposures that community residents may experience based on emissions from nearby permitted stationary sources. Varied results from actual monitoring, as compared with modeled data, also suggest problems with data accuracy, reducing the potential utility of modeling as a tool for conducting cumulative impact assessments.

RECOMMENDATIONS

- EPA should consult with state and local health and environmental agencies to address environmental justice concerns and identify high-priority areas where residents are exposed to large amounts of pollution.

- EPA should collect monitoring data from high-risk areas, and use this information as a tool for identifying potential health hazards and helping permit writers to develop appropriate terms and conditions for permits that will address environmental justice concerns. Where monitoring is not practical due to cost or other factors, modeling should be used to estimate impacts on high-priority areas, understanding that modeling is less precise than monitoring. Upon scientific peer review, EPA should utilize the National-Scale Air Toxics Assessment as a screening tool to identify potential high-priority areas where the agency will conduct a thorough examination of pollution sources.

- EPA should evaluate tools that have been developed by its regional and program offices, as well as by the Offices of Policy, Civil Rights, and Environmental Justice. From these evaluations, the agency should identify potential best practices to recommend when developing practical guidance documents about how permitting staffs can incorporate environmental justice into EPA permits nationwide. EPA's Science Advisory Board should review the most useful tools, once they are available, to ensure that the agency's approaches apply good science.

- EPA should work to ensure the accuracy of data on emissions and exposures in specific communities. The accuracy of all data, especially point-source location data for facilities, is critical given that the agency uses this information to analyze very localized pollution impacts, typically the primary concern of high-risk communities.

ENDNOTES

[1] Natural Research Council, Committee on Risk Assessment of Hazardous Air Pollutants, Board on Environmental Sciences and Technology, Commission on Life Sciences, *Science and Judgment in Risk Assessment* Washington, D.C.: National Academy Press (1994).

[2] Presidential /Congressional Commission on Risk Assessment and Risk Management, *Risk Assessment and Risk Management in Regulatory Decision-Making* Washington, D.C., (1997).

[3] Public Law 170, 104th Cong., 2d Sess.

[4] *Title VI, Civil Rights Act of 1964*, 42 U.S.C. Sec. 2000d *et seq.*

[5] Title VI Implementation Advisory Committee, *Report of the Title VI Implementation Advisory Committee: Next Steps for EPA, State, and Local Environmental Justice Programs* (March 1, 1999) 20.

[6] Texas Natural Resources Conservation Commission, Interview with staff (September 25, 2001).

[7] U.S. EPA, Science Policy Council, "Cumulative Risk Assessment-Planning and Scoping" (July 3, 1997).

[8] Carol Browner to Assistant Administrators, *et al.* Memorandum, "Cumulative Risk Assessment Guidance-Phase I Planning and Scoping" (July 3, 1997) 1.

[9] Ibid., 1.

[10] Ibid., 2.

[11] Reggie Harris, EPA Region III Environmental Justice Coordinator, Interview (November 7, 2001).

[12] U.S. EPA, Office of Pesticide Programs, *Public Comment Draft, Proposed Guidance on Cumulative Risk Assessment of Pesticide Chemicals That Have a Common Mechanism of Toxicity* (June 22, 2000).

[13] U.S. EPA, Office of Environmental Information, *IPB – National-Scale Air Toxics Assessment (NATA).* Available at http://www.epa.gov/ipbpages/current/v.1_bkup_10_24/237.htm.

[14] Industrial Economics, Inc., *Community-Specific Cumulative Exposure Assessment for Greenpoint/Williamsburg New York, Final Report* (Cambridge, Massachusetts: September 1999).

[15] Title VI Implementation Advisory Committee, *Report of the Title VI Implementation Advisory Committee: Next Steps for EPA, State, and Local Environmental Justice Programs* (March 1, 1999) 20.

[16] U.S. EPA, Office of Research & Development, National Center for Environmental Assessment, *Framework for Cumulative Risk Assessment."* Available at http://www.epa.gov/ncea/raf/frmwrkcra.htm.

[17] U.S. EPA, Science Advisory Board, *An SAB Report: Review of Disproportionate Impact Methodologies: A Review By The Integrated Human Exposure Committee Of The Science Advisory Board,* EPA-SAB-IHEC-99-007 (December 1998).

[18] Interview with Mike Callahan, Region VI Staff Scientist (September 24, 2001).

[19] U.S. EPA, Office of the Chief Financial Officer, *EPA Strategic Plan,* EPA/190-R-97-002 (September 1997) 17.

[20] U.S. EPA, "EPA Monitoring Study May Lead To Increased Testing For Air Toxics." *Inside E.P.A.*, Vol. 22, No. 45 (November 9, 2001) 5.

[21] Larry Starfield, Region VI, Interview (September 24, 2001).

[22] Environmental Law Institute, *Fresh Air: Innovative, State and Local programs for Improving Air Quality* (December 1997), 55-60.

[23] Starfield interview.

[24] U.S. EPA, Office of Environmental Information, *National-Scale Air Toxics Assessment*, Available at http://www.epa.gov//ipbpages/current/v.1_bkup_10_24/237.htm.

[25] Wilbert J. Wilson, personal correspondence (August 21, 2001).

[26] U.S. EPA Region V, *EPA's Cleveland Air Toxics Pilot Project – Home Page* (November 1, 2001). Available at http://www.epa.gov/cleveland.

[27] Industrial Economics, Inc., *Community-Specific Cumulative Exposure Assessment for Greenpoint/Williamsburg, New York, Final Report* (Cambridge, Massachusetts: September 1999).

[28] U.S. EPA, Region II, Community Resources, *Interim Environmental Justice Policy*, December 2000.

[29] Olivia Balandran, U.S. EPA Region VI, Environmental Justice Leader, Interview (September 24, 2001).

[30] U.S. EPA, *Part II, Environmental Protection Agency; Draft Title VI Guidance for EPA Assistance Recipients Administering Environmental Permitting Programs (Draft Recipient Guidance) and Draft Revised Guidance for Investigating Title VI Administrative Complaints Challenging Permits (draft Revised Investigation Guidance); Notice,* Fed. Reg. Vol. 65, No. 124 (June 27, 2000).

[31] Industrial Economics, *Community-Specific Cumulative Exposure Assessment for Greenpoint/Williamsburg, New York, Final Report* (Cambridge, Massachusetts: September 1999) 1-1.

[32] Ibid.

[33] U.S. EPA, Office of Cooperative Environmental Management, Report to the Title VI Implementation Advisory Committee, *Next Steps for EPA, State and Local Environment Justice Programs* (March 1, 1999) 16. Available at http://www.epa.gov/ocempage/nacept/titleVI/titlerpt.html.

[34] California Air Resources Board, *Neighborhood Assessment Program Work Plan* (June 30 2000). Available on the World Wide Web at http://www.arb.ca.gov/ch/napworkplan.htm.

[35] Ibid.

[36] Katherine Dawes, Personal Correspondence, *OPEI information for NAPA EJ Evaluation* (November 1, 2001).

[37] U.S. EPA, *Interagency Committee Selects Barrio Logan Community As An Environmental Justice Pilot Project* (November 13, 2000). Available at http://www.epa.gov/region09/features/barriologan/index.html.

[38] Northeast States for Coordinated Air Use Management (NESCAUM), *EPA Administrator Christine Whitman Joins In Announcing First Clean Air Communities Project* (August 6, 2001). Available at http://www.cleanaircommunities.org/press/080601-huntspoint.html.

[39] The National Academy of Public Administration, *Environment.gov: Transforming Environmental Protection for the 2Ist Century* (2000) and *Evaluating Environmental Progress: How EPA And The States Can Improve The Quality Of Enforcement And Compliance Information* (June 2001).

CHAPTER FIVE

EQUIPPING COMMUNITIES AND EPA STAFF FOR BETTER PUBLIC PARTICIPATION IN PERMITTING

FINDINGS

Finding 14: Many government officials, business representatives, and community activists believe that EPA's formal avenues for public participation in the permitting process are inadequate to address the concerns of disproportionately impacted communities. The public remains uninvolved until EPA has negotiated with applicants and resolved most of the permit questions.

Finding 15: To have a more effective voice in permit decisions, community group members need better training on how to participate in the process, resources to obtain technical help for more effective participation, and earlier notice about the proposed permit application. The last would allow them to become involved in negotiations with the applicant at the same time as EPA.

Finding 16: EPA has experimented with various ways of enhancing public participation, but these techniques are not yet standard operating procedure for the agency's permitting processes in the air, water, and waste programs.

Finding 17: Facilitated dialogues, using well-trained neutral third parties, can make significant contributions to resolving many community concerns about permitting, especially if they are conducted very early in the process.

Finding 18: Giving early notice to local officials about permit applications can enable them to consider such community concerns as odor, noise, traffic, and other issues that are outside EPA's jurisdiction, but that local agencies may have authority to address.

Finding 19: EPA technical assistance and facilitated dialogue resources for community groups regarding permitting are quite limited except in the Superfund program.

Finding 20: Disproportionately impacted community members want better access to technical information that will enable them to participate more effectively in negotiations about permit terms and conditions.

BACKGROUND

The Clean Air Act, the Clean Water Act, and the Resource Conservation and Recovery Act require that the public have a formal opportunity to comment on EPA draft permits. This opportunity typically takes place once EPA has prepared a draft permit. This often occurs several weeks or months after the original permit application was submitted to EPA. Environmental laws intend for these formal public comment opportunities to enhance the openness of permitting processes. Public comment on draft permits occurs too late in the process, however, to produce meaningful changes in many permits or to allow time for EPA dialogue with applicants and the affected communities. As a result, most public participation has not helped EPA to deal with citizen concerns about permits. Nor has it ensured that the best information is made available to permit writers, or reduced disputes between EPA and the affected communities.

In her August 9, 2001 memorandum reaffirming EPA's commitment to environmental justice, Administrator Christine Todd Whitman noted that this issue requires "ensuring greater public participation in the Agency's development and implementation of environmental regulations and policies."[1] Similarly, a National Environmental Policy Commission report recently stated: "Despite the numerous laws, mandates and directives by the federal government to involve the public in decision making, communities repeatedly expressed their frustration over their continued lack of involvement in decisions that impact their daily lives."[2] One of the four "Action Agenda" items developed by the federal Interagency Working Group on Environmental Justice calls on the participating agencies to "make government more accessible and responsive to communities."[3] Furthermore, in a December 2000 review of its public participation policy, EPA itself observed, "active public participation in EPA decision-making processes is critical to ensuring that the agency bases its decisions on the most pertinent information and creates workable long-term solutions for affected communities, industries, public health and the environment."[4] The agency then concluded, "to engage the public in this new century, EPA will need to reach out to a more diverse society, enhance public participation practices, and work more closely with our co-regulators."[5]

EPA's Superfund program, which supports redevelopment of potentially contaminated property through the "Brownfields" initiative, has emphasized the need to work constructively with the public. These public participation programs are predicated on providing early notice to communities about proposed projects, training EPA staff to work with communities, designating a specific community liaison official, and providing technical resources to communities for supporting their effective participation in the EPA decision-making process. A 1999 study of seven Brownfields redevelopment projects by EPA's Office of Solid Waste revealed that citizens at the sites did not file any Title VI civil rights complaints. The two most common factors cited for this result were early and meaningful community involvement, and redevelopment that creates benefits for the community. The study found,

> Each pilot has a unique community involvement approach or model, specifically designed for its community's political, geographic and organizational structure. While it is clear that models cannot simply be translated from one city to another, the case studies reveal promising components of various pilot activities that other pilots can use to help ensure sustained community involvement. These strategies include: 1) educating community representatives and other stakeholders; 2) institutionalizing the Brownfields decision-making process; 3) facilitating timely and clear decision-making with state officials; 4) making meetings/information accessible; and 5) creating and promoting trust through the use of neutral parties.[6]

Improving the capacity and opportunity for community groups to participate in the permitting process is an almost universally identified step toward achieving environmental justice. Public participation by itself is not the solution to environmental justice problems, but such problems cannot be resolved without improved public participation. The type and scale of public involvement may vary based on the nature of a specific permit application, but most basic aspects of participation should apply to all EPA permits. To address environmental justice concerns more effectively, EPA's permitting programs should include the public participation elements discussed below.

BUILDING COMMUNITY CAPACITY TO PARTICIPATE

Community members are not often familiar with when and how to participate in permitting processes. EPA-sponsored training for local communities, such as "The Proof is in the Permit" (developed by the New York Public Interest Research Group and implemented with community group input),[7] can build communities' capacity to play a more effective role. These types of courses can provide a clearer picture of how permitting works, including its limitations, and what kinds of information must be provided to influence EPA's decision on particular classes of permits.[8]

Increasing EPA's Resources for Community Assistance

EPA's financial costs and staff time increase when it expands the ability of individuals or communities to participate in permitting processes, provides technical services to aid communities, and directs more staff resources toward public participation. However, Academy research indicates that enhancing public participation is critical for EPA to improve its permitting processes, address environmental justice concerns, and resolve controversies so environmentally appropriate projects may proceed. Discussing environmental justice issues, one state official aptly noted that EPA and state environmental agencies over the past several years have significantly increased the resources devoted to technical and compliance assistance for regulated businesses. These efforts are important for achieving improved environmental results, yet EPA's resources for assisting and involving communities in permitting programs have not increased correspondingly.

Providing Earlier Opportunities to Participate

EPA's air, water, and RCRA permit programs provide formal opportunities for public participation. However, they usually occur late in the permitting process when most projects have been fully shaped, and when facility and EPA staff have reached agreement on permit conditions or changes to the original proposals. This late participation significantly limits the community's ability to influence the permit and analyze the project's potential effects. Moreover, because the public was not involved in the earlier stages, it may tend to view the permit applicant and EPA as allies. As a result, the community is more likely to challenge the permit and create costly, time-consuming delays, not believing that EPA would address their legitimate concerns. Although formal public comment processes are necessary and useful, they currently are too late and limited in many cases to provide EPA with an opportunity to address concerns appropriately.

Texas recently adopted legal requirements to notify the public when it receives a complete permit application.[9] This approach provides an opportunity for the public to comment at a stage when the environmental agency can take its comments into account as part of the give-and-take between the permit applicant and the agency staff. This is when the applicant may more easily be able to accept changes to the project design that will accommodate community concerns. In addition, Texas' approach allows for more extended contacts between the agency's permitting staff and members of the affected community. This early notice approach takes more time and has produced many more public comments to the environmental agency, yet there have been fewer challenges to final permit decisions thus far.

EPA does not have a statutory mandate for early notice of permit applications, but it has clear legal authority and discretion to expand public participation opportunities. The General Counsel's legal opinion noted the following finding by EPA's Environmental Appeals Board in Chemical Waste Management, Inc., 6 E.A.B. 66, 1995 WL 395962 (1995):

> When the Region has a basis to believe that operation of the facility may have a disproportionate impact on a minority or low-income segment of the affected community, the region should, as a matter of policy, exercise its discretion to assure early and ongoing opportunities for public involvement in the permitting process.[10]

This decision recognizes EPA's ability to notify communities at an early stage in the permitting process and to involve them in negotiations about permit conditions, even prior to the formal public comment period. The legal opinion also indicates that the agency may be able to mandate additional public participation requirements, conferring a legal right for early involvement in permits under RCRA and for permitting publicly owned treatment works under the Clean Water Act. [11]

BUILDING COMMUNITY RELATIONSHIPS AND TRUST

Working effectively with a community during the permitting process is significantly enhanced if the community already has an established solid level of trust with EPA's staff. Yet this circumstance is rare today, except with the Superfund program which has used community liaisons for several years. It may not be practical to have EPA liaisons for all communities, but the agency could assign them to high-priority disproportionately impacted communities and work with states to establish a similar function for other communities. This approach would allow EPA and participating states to identify and understand community concerns, and to consult with key opinion leaders in the community. It also would provide the community with clear points of contact for EPA and state environmental agencies (See Textbox, *NEJAC: Core Values and Guiding Principles for the Practice of Public Participation*).

NATIONAL ENVIRONMENTAL JUSTICE ADVISORY COUNCIL'S (NEJAC)

Core Values and Guiding Principles for the Practice of Public Participation

The following 14 items appear in the *Model Plan for Public Participation* (February 2000), developed by the Public Participation and Accountability Committee of NEJAC, a federal advisory committee to EPA.

1. People should have a say in decisions about actions which affect their lives.

2. Public participation includes the promise that the public's contribution will influence the decision.

3. The public participation process communicates the interests and meets the process needs of all participants.

4. The public participation process seeks out and facilitates the involvement of those potentially affected.

5. The public participation process involves participants in defining how they participate.

6. The public participation process communicates to participants how their input was, or was not, utilized.

7. The public participation process provides participants with the information they need to participate in a meaningful way.

8. Involve the public in decisions about actions which affect their lives.

9. Maintain honesty and integrity throughout the process.

10. Encourage early and active community participation.

11. Recognize community knowledge.

12. Use cross-cultural methods of communication.

13. Institutionalize meaningful public participation by acknowledging and formalizing the process.

14. Create mechanisms and measurements to ensure the effectiveness of public participation.

Items 1-7 were adopted from *Interact: The Journal of Public Participation*, Volume 2, Number 1, Spring 1996. Interact is published by the International Association of Public Participation Practitioners. Items 8-14 are from *The Guiding Principles for Public Participation*, developed by the NEJAC's Public Participation/Accountability Workgroup to ensure the early involvement of the public.

For more information, see http://es.epa.gov/oeca/oej/nejac/pdf/modelbk.pdf

Improving Staff Outreach Skills

Most staff, including permit writers, do not have readily honed public participation instincts, understanding, and skills upon arriving at EPA. However, working with the public has become increasingly essential to carry out their work and minimize costly, time-consuming disputes. Effective public involvement requires broad-based skills, such as listening to non-technical people, understanding how to communicate with external audiences, learning techniques to structure effective meetings, arranging for other public involvement opportunities, understanding the range of public engagement techniques that are available and how to choose among them, and appreciating valuable information that successful community involvement can impart.

Staff training aside, several EPA programs and regions are re-examining their human resource models to ascertain the need to hire staff with specific community involvement skills, and those who better represent the diverse populations they serve. The agency has numerous programs to address these issues, including the community involvement programs developed in the Superfund program and the agency's Community Involvement University[12] (See Textbox, *Community Involvement University*). Not all EPA permit writers have skills for working with communities, although many may be able to acquire them. It may be possible for a permit writer who lacks strong community involvement skills to work with colleagues who do.

COMMUNITY INVOLVEMENT UNIVERSITY

Community Involvement University (CIU) was established by the Community Involvement and Outreach Center in EPA's Office of Emergency and Remedial Response (OERR). CIU provides opportunities for EPA's regional Superfund team members to build skills needed for successful community cleanup efforts.

CIU offers different courses annually on community involvement, facilitation, and cross-cultural collaboration. CIU also coordinates with the Office of Solid Waste and Emergency Response (OSWER) Training Forum. The Training Forum manages training schedules and activities and operates a website (http://www.trainex.org), that provides information on numerous technical and scientific courses related to site or incident management.

CIU courses allow community involvement coordinators, remedial project managers, on-scene coordinators, and other specialists associated with Superfund cleanups to learn new skills, enhance old ones, and gain insights into working effectively with community members and others affected by Superfund cleanups.

Some of the courses offered by CIU include:

- Public Involvement: How to Communicate, Listen, and Work with our Public
- Leadership, Attitude, Function, and Style
- Media Relations Training
- Introduction to Community Involvement
- Managing the Psychological and Social Stress of Working in Superfund Communities
- Communicating in a Crisis: Tools you can use when there is no time to waste
- Mastering Meetings
- Basic Facilitation
- Working with Hostile Meetings and Difficult People
- Cross Cultural Effectiveness

For more information, see http://www.trainex.org/pdf/ciu_brochure.pdf

Providing Technical Support for Public Participation

Communities do not always trust the objectivity of EPA staff. In cases where difficult technical issues and significant community concerns exist, the public often wants its own experts who can analyze the facts and advise on the proposed permits. EPA has substantial experience providing technical assistance to communities involved with Superfund issues through Technical Assistance Grants or the "TAG" program.[13] However, there are some concerns about using the TAG program as a technical assistance for model permitting programs. From the community perspective, there can be complexities and long delays when applying for a TAG. From the government perspective, there is concern that TAG experts can exacerbate controversies, rather than help communities and EPA work better together. TAG is currently limited to Superfund sites, and no similar program exists for EPA's air, water, and other waste permitting programs (See Textbox, *Technical Assistance Grant Process*).

TECHNICAL ASSISTANCE GRANT PROCESS

Congress included provisions in the Superfund Reauthorization Act of 1986 to establish the Technical Assistance Grant (TAG) program. This program recognizes the importance of community participation and the need to involve citizens living near National Priorities List (NPL) sites, the most hazardous waste sites nationwide. TAGs are intended to promote community involvement in EPA's decisions about site-specific cleanup strategies under Superfund.

TAG's provide funding for community activities associated with participation in the decision-making process at eligible Superfund sites. Those activities may include obtaining technical assistance from their own scientists or other experts who can interpret scientific data and other information about the site. This assistance then allows communities to assess independently the technical aspects of an issue or pending action, rather than relying on the regulated community or EPA for their information. An initial grant up to $50,000 is available for any Superfund site that is on EPA's NPL, or is proposed to be on it where a response action has begun.

For more information, see http://www.epa.gov/superfund/tools/tag/whatis.htm.

Community groups can obtain technical support for permitting through Technical Outreach Services for Communities (TOSC), an EPA program.[14] TOSC is a service of the university-based Hazardous Substance Research Centers, funded by EPA and the Department of Defense. The services – provided through two universities located in each region – are focused on hazardous waste issues and include providing a base of fundamental scientific information; interpreting and summarizing reports; clarifying the regulatory process generally and site-

68

specifically; and addressing specific site contamination issues, including extent of contamination, contaminant dynamics, exposure, health, and ecological considerations, and potential remediation technologies. TOSC has proved useful to some environmental justice situations, but it has limits. First, the program has scarce resources and can only meet the needs of a few communities seeking assistance on technical issues. Second, only ten universities are involved in TOSC; thus, university experts may be outsiders to a community and not necessarily be more trusted than others (See Textbox, *Technical Outreach Services for Communities*).

TECHNICAL OUTREACH SERVICES FOR COMMUNITIES

The mission of the Technical Outreach Services for Communities (TOSC) program is to help communities with hazardous-substance pollution problems. By providing independent technical information and assistance, TOSC helps communities to better understand technical issues and to participate in environmental decisions.

TOSC is a service of the Hazardous Substance Research Centers (HSRC) program. Over thirty universities nationwide form a network of five HSRCs. Each HSRC serves two EPA regions.

Meaningful community participation in environmental decisions is most useful when community members understand the technical issues involved. The TOSC program gives power to communities through education and information.

Through TOSC, each regional HSRC works directly with local communities on hazardous-substance problems. Each center helps communities to understand the problems and create solutions. TOSC may also promote communication and dialogue among different groups with interests in the site.

Additionally, TOSC provides technical outreach to communities, by using new technologies and training, as well as the expertise of HSRC educators and researchers. This outreach supports the communities with the scientific and engineering information needed for participation in EPA's cleanup decisions.

Funding for the HSRCs is provided by EPA, the Department of Defense, the Department of Energy, and other federal and state agencies, participating universities, and private sources.

TOSC is designed to complement the technical assistance that EPA offers to communities through the Superfund Technical Assistance Grant (TAG) program. However, there are two key differences. First, unlike TAG, TOSC is not limited to sites on the National Priorities List. TOSC is available to many communities with hazardous-substance problems that are not otherwise eligible for TAG. Second, TOSC is not a grant program, and it is easier for informal community groups to access because there are no federal or incorporation requirements, as are common with TAG.

For more information, see
http://www.epa.gov/unix0008/community_resources/tosc/toschome.html

---

Offering Facilitated Dialogues

Various public involvement approaches have addressed community concerns about proposed new or modified facilities. One helpful technique for controversial situations has been facilitated dialogue, which uses a neutral third party to manage interactions among the community, a permit applicant, the regulatory agency, and other interested parties. This dialogue can be informal or involve formal dispute resolution processes like mediation. Such negotiations can address issues and propose solutions not identified in typical public meetings, hearings, or informal discussions with interested parties. Funding for mediation and other facilitated dialogue approaches is available through EPA's Office of Environmental Justice and a standing contract managed by the Office of Solid Waste and Emergency Response.[15] The agency's demand for dispute resolution services under that contract has skyrocketed from four work assignments during the initial five-year grant period to 206 during the most recent five-year grant period.[16]

Numerous issues relate to facilitated dialogues, including (1) the types of dialogue that are most useful for specific kinds of issues or disputes and when to use them, (2) how knowledgeable EPA staff are about "interest-based negotiation," (3) access to resources to ensure successful community participation in dialogues, (4) EPA program ability to access quickly facilitation/mediation resources, and (5) the availability of resources to fund dialogues other than those in the waste program. An evaluation of the value of collaborative efforts, currently underway through EPA's Office of Policy, Economics and Innovation, should answer some of these questions.[17]

EPA needs to document what it has learned from past uses of various dispute resolution methods, such as facilitated dialogues and more formal mediation. These experiences, together with a review of the relevant literature, should provide the agency with a rich set of information about when these tools are most useful. Based on this information, EPA should develop some guidance for its permitting programs on how to maximize the success of these dialogues in terms of timing, location, choice of facilitator, and identifying the appropriate participants.

EPA headquarters could make this information particularly useful for EPA permit writers and permitting program managers by developing a "decision tree" to determine when and how to use dialogue techniques. This decision tree should identify the factors for permit writers to consider when determining whether a facilitated dialogue would be useful in particular situations, including what type of dialogue would be most appropriate and the structure of the dialogue. EPA should then distribute this decision tree to all of its program and regional offices, along with information about other public involvement tools that have proven successful. Then EPA's permitting staff and managers would have the information they need to conduct efficient and effective public participation.

ENCOURAGING REGULATED ENTITIES TO EXPAND THEIR OUTREACH

An excellent way to address concerns about a permit application is for the applicant to meet and work with the community while the agency considers the application for permit renewal, modification, or a new facility. Indeed, a community involvement program is also often in the applicant's best interest. An industry association observed in a recent article on fast-track construction of energy facilities that:

> A proactive approach to plant siting public relations and education must take place at the earliest stages of the project. Moreover, the public relations program must take into account the committee's cultural sensitivities. Remember that your power plant is their neighbor.[18]

Many projects proceed with little opposition. Where opposition develops, however, the results can be very costly, in terms of time delays and public relations should the applicant lack a way to work with community groups. EPA has encouraged corporate good neighbor policies, including plans to involve communities early in any permitting process. For example, the Office of Solid Waste and Emergency Response publishes *Social Aspects of Siting RCRA Hazardous Waste Facilities*[19] (See Textbox, *Social Aspects of Siting*), which provides helpful information and advice to permit applicants on how to work with communities effectively.

SOCIAL ASPECTS OF SITING:
A CHECKLIST ON SITING FACILITIES FOR EPA AND INDUSTRY

Address the fundamentals:
- ✓ Integrate cultural/social and economic needs of a community into early site planning
- ✓ Establish partnerships with communities
- ✓ Take time to find out about a community's quality of life concerns
- ✓ Learn about environmental justice programs that may apply at the site

Be prepared to answer questions on:
- ✓ Routine environmental exposure
- ✓ Threat of spills and likelihood of exposure from accidental releases
- ✓ Evacuation routes and alternative routes
- ✓ Noise and odor
- ✓ Influence on outdoor activities
- ✓ Influence on development of neighboring property
- ✓ Devaluation of surrounding land and personal property
- ✓ Gardening and fishing activity nearby---recreational or subsistence
- ✓ Effect on property of cultural and social significance
- ✓ Displacement of existing jobs or potential for new jobs and skills match

Collect information on:
- ✓ Community boundaries---residential and commercial
- ✓ Demographics
- ✓ Education level of residents
- ✓ Cultural background and values of residents
- ✓ Actual land use
- ✓ Emissions from existing facilities, e.g., existing emission sources and cumulative impacts
- ✓ Environmental permitting history
- ✓ Key community members and institutions
- ✓ Existing contamination information
- ✓ Areas used by high-risk populations (schools, hospitals, recreation areas)
- ✓ History of all environmentally permitted activities
- ✓ Oral history of community's health
- ✓ Location of sites of special culture

Develop effective communication plan based on:
- ✓ How the community members communicate with each other
- ✓ How the community gets its information
- ✓ Building trust with a two-way, open dialogue, responding to all comments and questions
- ✓ Holding effective public meetings
- ✓ Early on, devising and using an effective outreach strategy
- ✓ Providing technical assistance to community members
- ✓ Reaching out before site selection

Source: U.S. EPA, Office of Solid Waste and Emergency Response, *Social Aspects of Siting RCRA Hazardous Waste Facilities* (April 2000), p.13.

EPA officials and several states indicated that they routinely urge applicants to work closely with communities surrounding their facilities. In addition to using its "bully pulpit," EPA could use other on going programs for the regulated community, such as small business assistance training programs,[20] to help companies understand the techniques and benefits for working with affected communities during the permitting process.

COMMUNICATING INFORMATION TO THE COMMUNITY

Communities must have accurate, timely, understandable, and complete information about facilities, emissions, and enforcement activities. This is critical to building trust and empowering the public so it can meaningfully participate in EPA's permitting processes. Just as formal participation procedures provide inadequate opportunities to the public in many permitting decisions, legal notices in newspapers and permit information made available in government offices are equally ineffective. A recent report prepared by the National Environmental Policy Commission has pointed out that:

> Resources should be made available for culturally competent outreach, including language translation and explanation of scientific and technical issues, meetings scheduled for times most available to the affected community, longer comment periods for major or high-risk or technically complicated sources, all with a goal of more meaningful public participation.[21]

During an electronic dialogue on public involvement in EPA decisions, a participant from the Southern Organizing Community for Economic and Social Justice observed that:

> use of a variety of outreach avenues is most effective (in reaching "fence-line" communities), radio and television public service announcements and talk shows, news stories, newspaper paid ads, public meetings and meetings with neighborhood and community organizations, open houses and the like.... Churches and libraries are good places to distribute information....[22]

EPA offices have experimented with various techniques to notify the public about pending actions and to provide people with easier access to understandable data. For example, Region V advocates interviews through one-on-one conversations, or small group meetings to inform the community on how it can become involved.[23] EPA's new GIS, "Window on My Environment" (See Textbox, *Window on My Environment*), allows the public to quickly find information on environmental releases and facilities in its neighborhood through the Internet.[24] Various other tools are identified in EPA's new guide, *"Public Involvement in Permitting"*[25] and in the Environmental Law Institute's study, *"Building Capacity to Participate in Environmental Protection Agency Activities: A Needs Assessment and Analysis."*[26]

WINDOW ON MY ENVIRONMENT

Window on My Environment (WME) is sponsored by EPA in partnership with federal, state, and local organizations. It is designed to improve the public's access to useful community-based environmental information. In connection with WME, EPA, the states, and other data sources are developing a comprehensive data exchange network that will compile environmental information for agencies' and public use.

WME is EPA's prototype of a geographical portal for integrating environmental information with local geography to answer public questions, examine critical problems, and discover potential solutions for environmental protection and human health issues.

WME was developed to incorporate new technology, environmental data, and information resources from EPA and other federal agencies, states, tribes and communities. In 2001, the demonstration phase will make WME more user-friendly, providing wider geographic coverage, live-streaming of data from partners, and greater breadth and depth of environmental data and information resources. Data standards, data quality, and consistency in reporting methods also are being refined as part of the WME pilot phase.

Current features of WME include:

- state-of-the-art interactive mapping tools
- data on ambient environmental conditions
- access to analytical and reporting tools
- local governmental services and contacts

When a user enters a specific location to be profiled, such as city/town and state or zip code, WME will display:

- An Interactive Map: the location of regulated facilities, monitoring sites, water bodies, community demographics, and three-dimensional views. Hotlinks are provided to state/federal information about these items

- Your Window: statistics about conditions in a specific area, including population density, country/urban area designations, and local watersheds/water bodies

- Your Environment: information from federal, state, and local partners on environmental issues such as air and water quality, watershed health, Superfund sites, fish advisories, polluted waters, and local services for protecting the environment

For more information, see http://www.epa.gov/enviro/wme

RECOMMENDATIONS

- EPA should expand its TAG and TOSC programs to offer more timely and accessible technical assistance to communities that need this support. This help would allow communities to participate effectively in EPA's air, water, and RCRA permitting processes, and in efforts to mitigate environmental risks in high-risk communities.

- Using its discretionary authority, EPA should adopt early notice procedures for communities once permit applications are complete, providing the name of an agency community liaison and soliciting community comments prior to negotiating the permit terms and conditions. EPA should expand these efforts beyond an experimental stage and should make them standard operating procedure.

- EPA should use community liaisons in some high-priority communities to assess how such an approach could improve communications and relationships with those communities.

- EPA should expand its public involvement training and offer significantly more training opportunities so that managers, permit writers, and other staff can develop stronger skills in outreach and public involvement techniques. This training is especially important for those who interact with, or make decisions about, the public.

- EPA's public participation resources, including staff training and technical assistance funding, should be expanded to provide greater balance in the amount of EPA support made available for assisting community groups and regulated businesses.

- EPA should use its facilitation and mediation experiences to create, publish, and widely disseminate a decision tree to help EPA staff decide when and under what circumstances dispute resolution and dialogue tools may be useful when dealing with environmental justice concerns. The agency also should make funding available in each region for the sole purpose of providing community and EPA access to facilitation/mediation resources. The decision tree can indicate when such approaches might be helpful in resolving permit controversies.

- EPA should continue to encourage regulated facilities and permit applicants to work with affected communities early in the permitting process, including publishing case studies that demonstrate the value of community involvement, offering outreach training as part of business assistance programs, and other techniques.

- EPA should use various mechanisms to provide information to communities about permit applications, such as more prominent newspaper notices; notices posted in local institutions including libraries, schools, and churches; establishment of a community liaison person; and web-based information. Also, EPA should expand its efforts to provide information in other languages as appropriate, and in easily understandable formats.

ENDNOTES

[1] Christine Todd Whitman to Assistant Administrators, *et al.*, memorandum, *EPA's Commitment to Environmental Justice* (August 9, 2001).

[2] National Environmental Policy Commission, *Report to the Congressional Black Caucus and Congressional Black Caucus Foundation Environmental Justice Braintrust* (September 28, 2001), 43.

[3] U.S. EPA, Office of Environmental Justice, *Integrated Federal Interagency Environmental Justice Action Agenda* (November 2000): 7.

[4] U.S. EPA, Office of Policy, Economics and Innovation, *Engaging the American People: A Review of EPA's Public Participation Policy and Regulations with Recommendations for Action* (December 2000), 1.

[5] Ibid.

[6] U.S. EPA, Office of Solid Waste and Emergency Response, *Brownfields Title VI Case Studies: Summary Report* (June 1999) 16.

[7] New York Public Interest Research Group, *The Proof is in the Permitting.*, Available at http://www.titlev.org/handbook.htm.

[8] Elizabeth Mullin, *The Art of Commenting: How to Influence Environmental Decisions with Effective Comments*, 2000. Environmental Law Institute.

[9] Texas Natural Resources Conservation Commission Interview with Staff (September 25, 2001).

[10] Gary S. Guzy to Steven A. Herman, Robert Perciasepe, Timothy Fields, Jr., and J, Charles Fox, Memorandum, "EPA Statutory and Regulatory Authorities Under Which Environmental Justice Issues may be Addressed in Permitting" (December 1, 2000), 2.

[11] Ibid., 4.

[12] U.S. EPA, Office of Emergency and Remedial Response, Community Involvement and Outreach Center, *Community Involvement University* (2001).

[13] U.S. EPA, *Technical Assistance Grants (TAG)*. Available at http://www.epa.gov/superfund/tools/tag/.

[14] U.S. EPA, *Technical Outreach Services for Communities.* Available at http://www.epa.gov/region08/community_resources/tosc/toschome.html.

[15] U.S. EPA, Conflict Prevention and Resolution Center, "Index." Available http://www.epa.gov/adr/index.html.

[16] National Environmental Policy Commission, *Report to the Congressional Black Caucus and Congressional Black Caucus Foundation Environmental Justice Braintrust* (September 28, 2001), 13.

[17] U.S. EPA, Office of Policy, Economics and Innovation, *Strategy for Evaluating the Environmental Justice Collaborative Model* (July 12, 2001).

[18] Edison Electric Institute, *Electric Perspectives* (March/April 2001), 4.

[19] U.S. EPA, Office of Solid Waste and Emergency Response, *Social Aspects of Siting RCRA Hazardous Waste Facilities*, EPA530-K-00-005 (April 2000).

[20] U.S. EPA Office of Air and Radiation and Office of Air Quality Planning and Standards Interviews with Staff (October 18, 2001).

[21] National Environmental Policy Commission, *Report to the Congressional Black Caucus and Congressional Black Caucus Foundation Environmental Justice Braintrust* (September 28, 2001) 48.

[22] www.network-democracy.org/epa-pip/archive/seq00242.html; see also Environmental Law Institute, *Libraries as a Community Resource for Environmental Information* (December 2000).

[23] U.S. EPA, Region V, *Interim Guidelines for Identifying and Addressing A Potential Environmental Justice Case* (June 1998): 24.

[24] U.S. EPA, *Window to My Environment,"* Available at http://www.epa.gov/enviro/wme/

[25] U.S. EPA, Office of Solid Waste and Emergency Response, *Public Involvement in Environmental Permits: A Reference Guide* (August 2000).

[26] Environmental Law Institute, *Building Capacity to Participate in Environmental Protection Agency Activities: A Needs Assessment and Analysis* (June 1999).

Please assess the following questions and items as you conduct your work.

The purpose of this Checklist is to raise awareness of possible environmental justice (EJ) issues and dynamics when working with communities or when working with statewide policies that affect the public's health or a community's environment.

Reviewing these items will help to further identify possible issues of concern, appropriate considerations, or actions for follow-up. *Going through them* will benefit you and your program. *Not going through these considerations* could make your and the agency's work less effective, and possibly expose the agency to liabilities.

> If known or suspected EJ issues are identified by going through this Checklist (or by any other means), consult your program's EJ subcommittee representative or John Ridgway, Ecology's EJ coordinator, (360) 407-6713, jrid461@ecy.wa.gov.

Overall, consider the "stakeholders."
Who are they and who's missing?

LOCATION & IMPACT

☑ **Who lives, works, or recreates closest to the facility/site/area of concern?**
This first step helps to physically define the "community" and everyone who's in it. Consider: Are all the area's residents and users aware of the work you're doing and its relationship to their environment? Are they represented? How?

☑ In general, a **one-mile radius** from the area of concern should be considered for residents, including housing, tribes, schools, other institutions, etc. *For soil contamination*, an area smaller than a mile's radius may be adequate. *For air releases,* where weather patterns usually matter, a larger area may be more appropriate to consider. *For water-related issues,* down stream, down gradient, a local aquifer's area, or perhaps the entire drainage basin may be the area to consider. *In a small town,* it may be best to address the entire town. Transportation problems associated with a given project (e.g., construction or operation-related traffic on the only road through town) may also be an issue that can go far beyond a mile's radius.

☑ For **statewide effects** (rules, policies, etc.), the goal is to actively solicit comments and participation from a full representation of the "community." Identifying those who might ordinarily be left out is not as clear-cut. The key: look for, invite, welcome, and assist diversity. Look to draw in those most likely to be affected by the rule, policy, or other Ecology-related activity. This may mean going into a variety of communities, at least informally, and talking with them to better understand if there is a probable or possible effect on them. Arranging a tour with someone who knows the community will help.

☑ **Cumulative effects.** What other environmental pollution or environmentally related activities are or have been taking place within a 1- to 2-mile radius of the area in question? What is the cumulative effect of those other sites?

☑ To help make up for what is not posted in the facility/site system, the lead for the project or issue will be expected to let people in other programs within the regional office know what they're embarking upon.
This can be easily done by a "send-all" e-mail within the respective office. The regional EJ subcommittee contact and/or lead Public Information Officer (PIO) will also help to identify who would be most appropriate within the office to notify. Contact Education and Outreach

> Start at Ecology's "Facility/Site" Web site:
> http://www.ecy.wa.gov/services/as/iss/fsweb/fshome.html. This will show much (but likely, not all) of what Ecology is tracking in the area.

Specialists in the regions (Toxics Cleanup, Water Quality, Air Quality Programs, etc.) who are doing on-the-ground public-involvement work. They are likely already involved with some (or many) of the groups who will need to be contacted and may have already established positive relationships with them.

☑ In terms of cumulative effects, here's a basic point to consider: if there are multiple sources of pollution in the immediate area of interest, the need increases for a public health specialist to help assess those factors. This person should be prepared for health-related questions and concerns from the community and the news media. Help bring that expertise in early, starting with the staff from local public-health districts. Other resources are also available: see the **Public Health** reference later in this list.

SEPA/NEPA

☑ **Should the State or National Environmental Policy Acts be considered?** SEPA may be the most appropriate and best opportunity or tool to consider important issues covered in this checklist, whether site-specific or on a statewide basis. It's possible that the applicant/business/entity that's triggering Ecology's review or involvement isn't necessarily looking for SEPA/NEPA considerations when they should be. Either way, check with Ecology's SEPA staff if you're not sure. They can help determine what needs to be considered and done in this regard.

> Patty Betts in the Shorelands and Environmental Assessment Program, (360) 407-6925, can also help with this.

TRIBES

> You can get assistance in understanding tribal interests, tribal reservations, potential impacts and how to best communicate with tribes by contacting Ecology's liaison with tribal governments, Tom Laurie, Inter-governmental Liaison, (360) 407-7017.

☑ **Tribal treaty reserved rights.** Twenty-one tribes within the state have off-reservation rights guaranteed by the United States through treaties under which the tribes ceded title to most of the land within the state. These treaty-reserved rights include the right to take fish and shellfish in "usual and accustomed areas" throughout most of the state for commercial and subsistence purposes. If the site/facility/action will affect fish or shellfish, it will likely affect one or more tribes.

☑ **Tribal lands.** If a facility/site/action will affect tribal lands, Indian reservations in particular, the appropriate tribal government needs to be contacted and kept informed. Indian reservations are an available layer in our geographic information system (GIS) mapping files.

CULTURE AND LANGUAGE

☑ **Subsistence and cultural users.** Are any resources affected by the site/facility/action used for subsistence or for cultural purposes? In addition to direct problems created by discharges or displacement, subsistence use may be affected by treatment options or cleanup levels. This can apply to fishing, hunting, and/or harvesting, and tribal and/or non-tribal communities. Many Southeast Asian (and other) residents in Washington have cultures and diets that use or consume local foods, plants, mushrooms, nuts, etc., that are not cultivated or protected or managed as a conventional "crop." The gathering and consumption of fish, aquatic life, herbs and plants within a local environment – and Ecology's environmental work in the same water body or area can easily be related to subsistence issues. For more information about the relationships between subsistence consumption, toxicity exposure, and public health, see the **Public Health** reference later in this list.

☑ **Communication/language barriers**. Are there one or more notable non-English-speaking populations that may be part of the area or community in consideration? Regardless of the predominant language(s), is illiteracy an issue? Are your messages getting to those who need to see or hear them? The standard requirement to post notices in the legal page of the predominant newspaper of the region is not effective communication by itself.

☑ Notices at laundry facilities, homeless shelters, employment offices, food banks, post offices, bus stops/transit stations, and local radio stations will likely reach many more low-income or migrant residents. Also, churches, playgrounds, parks, health clinics, grocery stores, and community centers are effective places to consider for printed messages. Flyer inserts in newspapers specific to the culture (i.e., Latino, Vietnamese papers, etc.) or notices sent via school district cultural programs are also very effective. Notices in these locations also inform employees as much as the general public who goes there.

☑ **Cultural barriers**. What potential cultural barriers should be considered? Local residents from other cultures often don't trust the government, including meetings in government buildings. (This is not to imply that any local resident necessarily *does* trust a government meeting in a government building.)

> Ecology has an outstanding responsive, field-proven, translation resource for print, meetings and other needs. The "Multi-lingual Interpretation and Translation Teams" (MITT) work in Chinese, Spanish, Vietnamese and Korean. Don't hesitate to use this resource at http://aww.ecology.ecy.wa.gov /mitt/. If other languages are needed, including signing for the deaf, contact your EJ representative. And don't forget to add Ecology's TDD (Telecommunication Device for the Deaf) phone numbers to your notices.

MEETINGS

☑ **Non-government buildings**. It's perfectly acceptable, and in some cases it may be to an advantage, to conduct Ecology public meetings or events in non-governmental (or less traditional) buildings – provided that such locations still meet Americans with Disability Act requirements. Doing this may diminish or remove some cultural barriers, thus increasing attendance and participation. Schools, churches, tribal centers, fire stations, granges, community centers (formal or otherwise) are some suggested examples. Using a community hall may be the easiest and best thing you can do to create a welcoming meeting (for Ecology as well as the community) with good participation. People are more likely to come if they know the location as "their" community center – as compared to a place of bureaucrats and regulations.

☑ **Tables partially blocking entrances with sign-in sheets can be intimidating**. It's good to have an Ecology person at the entrance to welcome folks but try to not separate yourself with a table from those coming in. Consider placing the table along a wall; you won't be tempted to sit behind it and it won't be in the way. And don't feel compelled to require a sign-in. If someone does not wish to sign in, welcome him or her anyway. Let him/her know that his/her name and address is respectfully requested so we can send follow-up information related to the meeting's topic. If someone wishes an Ecology reply to his or her comment or question, a name and mailing address would be needed, of course. We appreciate having names to help know how many people attended the meeting. A list also helps show other visitors and meeting managers how many people intend to comment. If formal comments are being taken, a list of the names of those wishing to comment may be requested before the comment period starts (not necessarily before the meeting starts) to establish the order of speakers. However, the law doesn't require one's name to be on a list in order to have the right to walk up and comment at the last minute if there's time. Typically, a speaker's name is requested (to be given verbally) at the time the comment is given. **The point is, signing an attendance sheet is not required for admittance or participation in a public meeting.**

☑ **Check with locals (church leaders, teachers, community center staff, health clinic staff, etc.) to learn more about cultural factors.** They will likely be good resources to help draw local interest and participation.

☑ **Local meetings**. Are these events accessible? For meetings/hearings/workshops/other Ecology-sponsored public events, ensure accessibility to the greatest extent practicable. This applies not only to the Americans with Disability Act (ADA), but also to timing and geographic location. Low-income individuals seldom work 8-5 and often don't have a car. Consider these people who depend on public transit.

☑ Site the meeting as close as possible to those most likely to be affected. Would a Saturday event draw a broader (more diverse/more participatory) group, including younger people? Does a bus route serve the location? If so, does it run late enough in the evening to get folks home after the meeting? Could your meeting(s) take place at an already scheduled community event (that's open to all and appropriate for ADA considerations)? This may be where locally involved interests are more likely to attend and feel welcome to participate. Are you better off going to smaller venues (churches, schools, community service centers) or individual homes and talking face to face?

> Ecology has a very good resource to show which public facilities, beyond the traditional, are ADA accessible. Facility and Meeting Guidelines – Americans with Disability Act (ADA) Requirements, publication #97-701, should be reviewed for any kind of public meeting that Ecology is going to conduct or sponsor. It includes, by county, facilities that have already been certified to meet ADA requirements.

☑ **Types of meetings**: open houses, workshops, community forums and roundtables. Can each imply (and actually be) a less formal and more participatory event than a "meeting"? With the exception of formal hearings required by law, these other kinds of public events may likely bring a much better representation of the general public simply because of the descriptive name. Better yet, a real "open house" (even if not in an Ecology building) will encourage people to come any time during the event without the expectation that one has to be there from the start to the finish. This may also improve attendance, outreach, communication, and common understanding – which *is* the goal. An open house may require additional staff, but more people will be able to talk one-on-one with Ecology experts without having to wait or risk intimidation by speaking publicly (often into a microphone).

RESOURCES TO OVERCOME BARRIERS

☑ **Local expertise.** What and where are the effective networks for communicating within a community? These will likely include several of the following: schools (principals and teachers), local newspaper reporters, local radio stations, church leaders, multi-denominational organizations, community centers (their "events" organizers), community health centers (doctors *and* nurses), local government entities, libraries, environmental groups, etc. This is important to assess because they can be very good resources for answering some of the questions above. They may also be more effective (and less traditional) resources that can help get our message out. These resources may also help get the community's message(s) back to us. They can help answer our questions, provide us with quality comments, and bring broader public participation to our work.

☑ **Governmental barriers**. Who's doing what? Do we know who are all the regulatory and governmental entities at play in the issue we're dealing with, including their representatives? Are we coordinating with them? Does the community know who all the players are and how to contact them? Are we helping them understand what Ecology's role is in relation to the other, topic-related entities (EPA, city/county, local air authority, local public health, state public health, etc.)? Are we clearly stating what we're able to address and why? Not sure? Work to find this out as soon as possible. Invite these other governmental entities' participation, in writing as well as more personally. You don't have to do it all, but help introduce and explain their respective role(s) to all interested and affected parties.

> Grants to the community may be available through the federal or state government and possibly some private sources; look into this early. If relevant, check with your local EPA counterpart or Ecology's Solid Waste & Financial Assistance (SWFA) Program for additional information. Ellen Caywood within the SWFA Program, (360) 407-6132 is a good resource on this.

☑ **Technical and financial barriers.** Are the communities realistically prepared to understand the technical issues? Could they benefit from having technical expertise working with and/or for them (e.g., a geohydrologist, a public health official, a toxicologist, air pollution or regulatory expertise, etc.)? Limited grant dollars may be available to local governments or non-governmental groups for addressing specific environmental issues. The key is to determine this early enough to keep bureaucratic time constraints from getting in the way.

☑ **What cost-related issues could hamper a community's ability to participate with Ecology's activities?** These may include costs for transportation to Ecology meetings (and back home) or childcare costs to attend meetings. If you're relying on an Ecology (or any other) Web site for outreach to the public, confirm that Internet access is available and free at the local library (and check the ability to print and take materials home – is printing free?). Even then, don't assume everyone will use the Internet or is computer literate.

PUBLIC HEALTH

☑ **Identify public health risk. What's the connection to the local community's (public and environmental) health? Are there highly at-risk populations nearby, such as facilities for children or seniors or migrant workers?** Are local health district officials aware of the issue(s)? What about the Washington State Department of Health (DOH)? If you're not sure, call local health districts first to find out what they know and what they may be interested in knowing. There's a good chance that the environmental health expert(s) within the local health district office will know who, if anyone, would be interested or already involved in such matters.

☑ Formally **invite public health participation** with (or at least review of) your work if there is any chance of public health concerns. At the state DOH, hopefully an appropriate person to contact will be known by the staff you contact at the local health department. Be sure to let the local and state public health contacts know (in writing – at least by e-mail) of each other and your contact with both.

> If public health or toxicity problems are a suspected issue, there are (currently) at least six trained toxicologists within Ecology. Leslie Keill, (360) 407-6851, is an expert on fish-consumption issues. Cheryl Niemi, (360) 407-6440, is an expert on statewide water-quality toxicology issues. The other toxicologists include Craig McCormack, (360) 407-7193, Dave Bradley, (360) 407-6907, and Damon Delistraty, (509) 456-6362. Each is a good resource to help determine if a particular Ecology activity warrants more attention from a human toxicity perspective.

☑ Don't forget that other general experts on public health include the public. The public may be the most able to provide specific and/or unique public health profiles within their community, beyond what the government is aware of. Just because they're not doctors or public health officials doesn't mean they're not acutely aware of the health-related information that could be of particular value to Ecology's work and the community.

SUSTAINABILITY

☑ **What are the longer-term implications (that are reasonable to assume) for the local community's sustainable health in relation to the action with which Ecology's involved?** Is Ecology taking those implications into account? What assurances, if any, do local residents have that Ecology's work (permit, cleanup plan, new rule, etc.) will not harm them (or harm them disproportionately) in the future? What is the local public health department or official's perspective on this? They are often (but not always) much better prepared than we are to address these health-related questions, but we have to help them know what's there to assess. Again, invite these public health experts into your work early (and document such invitations).

ZONING

☑ This is clearly a major factor in many of the EJ dynamics within a community, and one that Ecology has very little, if any, control over. In the context of sustainability, **it may be wise to work with local zoning/planning authorities early and often** because they may have much more capacity to take cumulative environmental information into account regarding a community's long-term environmental health. This is also true for decisions about where residents and businesses are zoned relative to one another. Is it sustainable? You may not be able to answer the question, but at least in terms of environmental impact, it's a good idea to ask it and see where it leads you. (11/01)

APPENDIX B

PANEL AND STAFF BIOGRAPHIES

PANEL

Philip J. Rutledge, *Chair* - Professor Emeritus School of Public and Environmental Affairs and former Special Assistant to the President, Indiana University. Former Director, Department of Human Resources, District of Columbia; Professor of Public Administration, Howard University; Director of Policy Analysis, National League of Cities and U.S. Conference of Mayors; Deputy Administrator, Social and Rehabilitation Service, U.S. Department of Health, Education and Welfare; Deputy Manpower Administrator, U.S. Department of Labor.

A. James Barnes – Professor and former Dean, School of Public and Environmental Affairs, and Professor, School of Law, Indiana University. Former positions with the U.S. Environmental Protection Agency: Deputy Administrator; General Counsel; Special Assistant to Administrator/Chief of Staff. Former General Counsel, U.S. Department of Agriculture; Partner, Beveridge & Diamond; Campaign Manager, Governor William G. Milliken (Michigan); Assistant to Deputy Attorney General and Special Assistant/Trial Attorney, U.S. Department of Justice.

Jonathan B. Howes - Special Assistant to the Chancellor and Professor of Planning and Policy, University of North Carolina at Chapel Hill. Former Secretary, Department of Environment, Health and Natural Resources (DEHNR), State of North Carolina; Research Professor and Director, Center for Urban and Regional Planning, University of North Carolina; Mayor, Town of Chapel Hill; Director, Urban Policy Center, Urban America, Inc.; Director, State and Local Planning Assistance, U.S. Department of Housing and Urban Development.

Valerie Lemmie - City Manager, City of Dayton, Ohio. Former City Manager, City of Petersburg, Virginia; Director, Department of Environmental Services, City of Arlington, Virginia; Assistant Professor, Howard University. Former positions with the Washington, D.C. Government: Deputy Director, Department of Consumer/Regulatory Affairs; Assistant to the Director, Department of Consumer/Regulatory Affairs; Project Director, Minority Business Development Services, One America, Inc; Special Assistant, Office of Business and Economic Development; Financial Policy Analyst/Course Manager, Office of Comptroller, Labor Department (on assignment from Kansas City, Missouri).

David Mora - City Manager, Salinas, California. Former City Manager, Oxnard, California; Manager, Los Gatos, California. Increasingly responsible positions with Santa Barbara, California, including: Director, Community Relations; Assistant to City Administrator; Deputy City Administrator.

James Murley - Director, Joint Center for Environmental and Urban Problems, Florida Atlantic University. Former Secretary and Director, Division of Resource Planning and Management, Department of Community Affairs, State of Florida; Executive Director, 1000 Friends of Florida. Former positions with the National Oceanic and Atmospheric Administration, U.S. Department of Commerce: Director, Coastal Program Office, Office of Coastal Zone Management (OCZM); Congressional Officer; Gulf Coast Regional Manager, OCZM.

Eddie Williams - President, Joint Center for Political and Economic Studies. Fortner Vice President for Public Affairs and Director, Center for Policy Study, The University of Chicago; Foreign Service Reserve Officer, U.S. Department of State; Staff Assistant, U.S. Senate Committee on Foreign Relations.

STAFF

Suellen Terrill Keiner – *Director*, The Center for the Economy and the Environment, National Academy of Public Administration. Former Senior Attorney and Director, Program on Environment, Governance and Management, the Environmental Law Institute; Director of Litigation, the Environmental Policy Institute; Assistant Solicitor and Deputy Assistant Secretary for Energy and Minerals, U.S. Department of Interior; Natural Resources Consultant, Council of State Planning Agencies; Attorney representing environmental and civil rights groups in citizen suits.

William P. Shields - *Communications Associate*, Office of Communications, National Academy of Public Administration; Adjunct Professor in Government, American University. Former Program Coordinator and Research Assistant, American University; Mayoral Writer, Executive Office of the Mayor of Providence, Rhode Island.

LeRoy (Lee) Paddock - *Senior Consultant*, Principal, Paddock Environmental Research and Consulting; Visiting Scholar, Environmental Law Institute. Former Director of Environmental Policy, Minnesota Attorney General's Office; Senior Environmental Counsel, National Association of Attorneys General; Assistant Attorney General, Minnesota Attorney General's Office.

Richard J. Lazarus – *Senior Consultant*, Center for the Economy and the Environment, National Academy of Public Administration; Woodrow Wilson Fellow, Woodrow Wilson International Center for Scholars; Professor of Law, Georgetown University Law Center; former Professor of Law at the University of Texas Law School, Northwestern University School of Law, George Washington University National Law Center, and Indiana University (Bloomington); Office of the President-Elect Transition Team for the U.S. Department of Justice; Assistant to the Solicitor General, U.S. Department of Justice; Attorney, U.S. Department of Justice.

Ann E. Goode – *Senior Consultant*, Center for the Economy and Environment, National Academy of Public Administration; Environmental Protection Agency: Acting Deputy Administrator, Office of Air and Radiation; Director, Office of Civil Rights; Chief of Staff, Office of Air and Radiation; Assistant Director for Regional Affairs, Office of Atmospheric Programs. Special Assistant to the Director, U.S. Commission on Civil Rights; Staff Associate, National Research Council.

Mark Hertko - *Research Assistant*, Center for the Economy and Environment, National Academy of Public Administration.

Stacey Keaton - *Research Assistant*, Center for the Economy and Environment, National Academy of Public Administration.

Veronica Lenegan - *Research Assistant*, Center for the Economy and Environment, National Academy of Public Administration.

Charlene Walsh - *Administrative Assistant*, Center for the Economy and Environment, National Academy of Public Administration.

BIBLIOGRAPHY

Balandran, Olivia. U.S. EPA Region VI, Environmental Justice Leader. Interview, September 24, 2001.

Browner, Carol M., to Assistant Administrators, *et al.* Memorandum. *Cumulative Risk Assessment Guidance-Phase I Planning and Scoping.* July 3, 1997.

Browner, Carol M. *EPA's Environmental Justice Strategy.* April 3, 1995.

California Air Resources Board. "Neighborhood Assessment Program Work Plan." June 30, 2000. Available at http://www.arb.ca.gov/ch/napworkplan.htm.

Callahan, Michael A. U.S. EPA Region VI, Staff Scientist. Interview, September 24, 2001.

Council on Environmental Quality. *Environmental Justice: Guidance Under the National Environmental Policy Act.* 1997.

Dawes, Katherine. U.S. EPA, Office of Environmental Policy Innovation, Evaluation Support Division. Personal correspondence. "OPEI information on NAPA EJ Evaluation." November 1, 2001.

Edison Electric Institute. *Electric Perspectives.* March/April 2001.

Environmental Law Institute. *Building Capacity to Participate in Environmental Protection Agency Activities: A Needs Assessment and Analysis.* June 1999.

Environmental Law Institute. *Fresh Air: Innovative State and Local Programs for Improving Air Quality.* December 1997.

Environmental Law Institute. *Libraries as a Community Resource for Environmental Information.* December 2000.

Executive Order 12898. *Federal Actions to Address Environmental Justice in Minority Populations and Low Income Populations.* 1994.

Guzy, Gary S., to Steven A. Herman, Robert Perciasepe, Timothy Fields, Jr. and J. Charles Fox, Memorandum. *EPA Statutory Authorities Under Which Environmental Justice Issues May Be Addressed in Permitting.* December 1, 2000.

Harris, Reggie. U.S. EPA Region III, Environmental Justice Coordinator. Interview, November 7, 2001.

Hill, Barry E. U.S. EPA, Office of Environmental Justice. Personal Correspondence, November 13, 2001.

Industrial Economics, Inc. *Community-Specific Cumulative Exposure Assessment for Greenpoint/Williamsburg, New York, Final Report.* Cambridge, Massachusetts. September 1999.

Inside EPA. "EPA Monitoring May Lead To Increased Testing For Air Toxics." Vol. 22, No. 45 (November 9, 2001): 5.

Knauf Fiber Glass, GmbH. PSD Appeal Nos. 99-8 through 99-72. Environmental Appeals Board. Decided March 14, 2000.

Laws, Elliott P., to Director, Office of Emergency and Remedial Response, *et al.* Memorandum. *Integration of Environmental Justice Into OSWER Policy, Guidance, and Regulatory Development.* September 21, 1994.

Lazarus, Richard J. "Integrating Environmental Justice Into Environmental Permitting Decisions." Presentation before the Environmental Justice Panel of the National Academy of Public Administration. June 14, 2001.

Lazarus, Richard J., and Stephanie Tai. "Integrating Environmental Justice into EPA Permitting Authority." *Ecology Law Quarterly* (Volume 26, 1999): 617-678.

Mullin, Elizabeth. *The Art of Commenting: How to Influence Environmental Decisions with Effective Comments.* Environmental Law Institute, 2000.

National Academy of Public Administration. *Environment.gov: Transforming Environmental Protection for the 21st Century.* Washington, D.C.: 2000.

National Academy of Public Administration. *Environment.gov: Transforming Environmental Protection for the 21st Century, Research Papers 11-17, Vol III.* Washington, D.C.: 2000.

National Academy of Public Administration. *Evaluating Environmental Progress: How the EPA and the States Can Improve the Quality of Enforcement and Compliance Information.* June 2001.

National Academy of Public Administration. *Resolving the Paradox of Environmental Protection: An Agenda for Congress, EPA, & the States.* Washington, D.C.: 1997.

National Academy of Public Administration. *Setting Priorities, Getting Results: A New Direction For EPA.* Washington, D.C.: 1995.

National Environmental Justice Advisory Council to Carol Browner. Letter. *Environmental Justice in the Permitting Process.* August 3, 2000.

National Environmental Justice Advisory Council. *Environmental Justice in the Permitting Process: A Report from the National Environmental Justice Advisory Council's Public Meeting on Environmental Permitting—Arlington, Virginia November 30-December 2, 1999.* EPA/300-R-00-004. July 2000.

National Environmental Justice Council Charter. July 29,1999. Available at http://es.epa.gov/oeca/main/ej/nejac/charter.html.

National Environmental Policy Commission. *Report to the Congressional Black Caucus and Congressional Black Caucus Foundation Environmental Justice Braintrust.* September 28, 2001.

Natural Research Council, Committee on Risk Assessment of Hazardous Air Pollutants, Board on Environmental Sciences and Technology, Commission on Life Sciences. *Science and Judgment in Risk Assessment.* Washington, D.C.: National Academy Press. 1994.

New York Public Interest Research Group. *The Proof is in the Permit: How to Make Sure A Facility In Your Community Gets An Effective Title V Air Pollution Permit.* 2000. Available at http://www.titlev.org/handbook.htm.

Northeast States for Coordinated Air Use Management (NESCAUM). *EPA Administrator Christine Whitman Joins In Announcing First Clean Air Communities Project.* August 6, 2001. Available at http://www.cleanaircommunities.org/press/080601-huntspoint.html.

Presidential/Congressional Commission on Risk Assessment and Risk Management. *Risk Assessment and Risk Management in Regulatory Decision-Making.* Washington, D.C.: 1997.

Public Law 170, 104th Cong., 2d sess. *Food Quality Protection Act of 1996.*

Starfield, Lawrence. U.S. EPA Region VI, Acting Deputy Regional Administrator. Interview, September 24, 2001.

Targ, Nicholas. U.S. EPA, Office of Environmental Justice. Interview, November 13, 2001.

Texas Natural Resources Conservation Commission. Jody Henneke, *et al.* Interviews, September 25, 2001.

Title VI Implementation Advisory Committee. *Report of the Title VI Implementation Advisory Committee: Next Steps for EPA, State, and Local Environmental Justice Programs.* March 1, 1999.

Title VI, *Civil Rights Act of 1964.* 42 U.S.C., Sec. 2000d *et seq.*

U.S. EPA. "Environmental Equity: EPA's Position, Protection Should Be Applied Fairly." *EPA Journal* (March/April 1992).

U.S. EPA, *Environmental Justice Homepage.* Available at http://www.epa.gov/swerosps/ej/index.html#ejhist.

U.S. EPA. *Environmental Protection Agency Environmental Justice 1994 Annual Report.* 1995.

U.S. EPA. "Interagency Committee Selects Barrio Logan Community As An Environmental Justice Pilot Project." November 13, 2000. Available at http://www.epa.gov/region09/features/barriologan/index.html.

U.S. EPA. "Part II, Environmental Protection Agency; Draft Title VI Guidance for EPA Assistance Recipients Administering Environmental Permitting Programs (Draft Recipient Guidance) and Draft Revised Guidance for Investigating Title VI Administrative Complaints Challenging Permits (draft Revised Investigation Guidance); Notice." Fed. Reg. Vol. 65, No. 124. June 27, 2000.

U.S. EPA. *Technical Assistance Grants* (TAG). Available at http://www.epa.gov/superfund/tools/tag/.

U.S. EPA. *Technical Outreach Services for Communities.* Available at http://www.epa.gov/region08/community_resources/tosc/toschome.html.

U.S. EPA. *Window to My Environment.* Available at http://www.epa.gov/enviro/wme/.

U.S. EPA, Conflict Prevention and Resolution Center. *Index.* Available at http://www.epa.gov/adr/index.html.

U.S. EPA, Office of Air and Radiation. *Improving Air Quality with Economic Incentive Programs.* EPA-452/R-01-001. January 2001.

U.S. EPA, Office of Air and Radiation, and Office of Air Quality Planning and Standards. William T. Harnett, *et al.* Interviews, October 18, 2001.

U.S. EPA, Office of Air Quality Planning and Standards, Technology and Transfer Network. *The National Training Workshop on Local Urban Air Toxics Assessment and Reduction Strategies.* 1999. Available at http://www.epa.gov/ttn/atw/wks/mainwks.html.

U.S. EPA, Office of the Chief Financial Officer. *EPA Strategic Plan.* EPA/190-R-97-002. September 1997.

U.S. EPA, Office of Cooperative Environmental Management. Report to the Title VI Implementation Advisory Committee, *Next Steps for EPA, State and Local Environment Justice Programs.* March 1, 1999. Available at http://www.epa.gov/ocempage/nacept/titleVI/titlerpt.html.

U.S. EPA, Office of Emergency and Remedial Response, Community Involvement and Outreach Center. *Community Involvement University.* 2001.

U.S. EPA, Office of Enforcement and Compliance Assurance. *1998 Environmental Justice Biennial Report: Moving Towards Collaborative and Constructive Problem-Solving.* EPA 300/R-00-004. July 2000.

U.S. EPA, Office of Enforcement and Compliance Assurance. *Environmental Justice Query Mapper.* 2001. Available at http://es.epa.gov/oeca/main/ej/ejmapper/.

U.S. EPA, Office of Enforcement and Compliance Assurance. *Small Grants Program Application Guidance FY 2000.* October 2001.

U.S. EPA, Office of Environmental Information. "National-Scale Air Toxics Assessment." Date not given. Available at http://www.epa.gov//ipbpages/current/v.1_bkup_10_24/237.htm.

U.S. EPA, Office of Environmental Justice. *Environmental Justice Small Grants Program: Emerging Tools for Local Problem-Solving.* 1999.

U.S. EPA, Office of Environmental Justice. *Environmental Justice Strategy: Executive Order 12898.* 1995.

U.S. EPA, Office of Environmental Justice. *Guidance to Assessing and Addressing Allegations of Environmental Injustice: Working Draft.* January 10, 2001.

U.S. EPA, Office of Environmental Justice. *Integrated Federal Interagency Environmental Justice Action Agenda.* November 2000.

U.S. EPA, Office of Pesticide Programs. *Public Comment Draft, Proposed Guidance on Cumulative Risk Assessment of Pesticide Chemicals That Have a Common Mechanism of Toxicity.* June 22, 2000.

U.S. EPA, Office of Policy, Economics and Innovation. *Engaging the American People: A Review of EPA's Public Participation Policy and Regulations with Recommendations for Action.* December 2000.

U.S. EPA, Office of Policy, Economics and Innovation. *Strategy for Evaluating the Environmental Justice Collaborative Model.* July 12, 2001.

U.S. EPA, Office of Policy, Economics and Innovation. *Work Related to Environmental Justice (2000-2001).* October 31, 2001.

U.S. EPA, Office of Policy, Planning and Evaluation. *Environmental Equity: Reducing Risk for All Communities, Vol. I and II.* EPA A230-R-92-008A. June 1992.

U.S. EPA, Office of Research & Development, National Center for Environmental Assessment. *Framework for Cumulative Risk Assessment.* Date not given. Available at http://www.epa.gov/ncea/raf/frmwrkcra.htm.

U.S. EPA, Office of Solid Waste and Emergency Response. *Brownfields Title VI Case Studies: Summary Report.* June 1999.

U.S. EPA Office of Solid Waste and Emergency Response. *OSW Environmental Justice Program Strategy.* Date not given. Available at http://www.epa.gov/osw/ej/.

U.S. EPA, Office of Solid Waste and Emergency Response. *Public Involvement in Environmental Permits: A Reference Guide.* August 2000.

U.S. EPA, Office of Solid Waste and Emergency Response. *Social Aspects of Siting RCRA Hazardous Waste Facilities.* EPA530-K-00-005. April 2000.

U.S. EPA, Office of Solid Waste and Emergency Response. *Waste Transfer Stations: Involved Citizens Make the Difference.* EPA530-K-01-003. January 2001.

U.S. EPA, Region II, Community Resources. *Interim Environmental Justice Policy.* December 2000.

U.S. EPA Region V. "EPA's Cleveland Air Toxics Pilot Project – Home Page." November 1, 2001. Available at http://www.epa.gov/cleveland.

U.S EPA, Region V. *Interim Guidelines for Identifying and Addressing A Potential Environmental Justice Case.* June 1998.

U.S. EPA, Science Advisory Board. *An SAB Report: Review of Disproportionate Impact Methodologies: A Review By The Integrated Human Exposure Committee (IHEC) Of The Science Advisory Board (SAB).* EPA-SAB-IHEC-99-007. December 1998.

U.S. EPA, Science Policy Council. *Cumulative Risk Assessment-Planning and Scoping.* July 3, 1997.

Wells, Suzanne and Pat Carey. U.S. EPA, Office of Solid Waste and Emergency Response. Interview, September 10, 2001.

Whitman, Christine Todd, Memorandum to Assistant Administrators, *et al. EPA's Commitment to Environmental Justice.* August 9, 2001.

Wilson, Wilbert J. U.S. EPA, Office of Air and Radiation. Personal correspondence, August 21, 2001.

Wood, Anna. U.S. EPA, Office of Air and Radiation. Personal correspondence, November 7, 2001.

ADDITIONAL RESOURCES

Briggum, Sue, Waste Management. *Environmental Justice and Permitting.* Presentation for the National Academy of Public Administration Environmental Justice Panel. 2001.

California Council for Environmental and Economic Balance. *CCEEB's Comments on EPA's Draft Title VI Guidance for EPA Assistance Recipients Administering Environmental Permitting Programs and Draft Revised Guidance for Investigating Title VI Administrative Complaints Challenging Permits.* 2000.

Center for Policy Alternatives. *EJ Legislation in the States.* 1996.

Clean Air Communities. *New Collaborative Commits $5 Million for Clean Air Projects in New York City's Impacted Communities.* 2000.

Clean Water Act. 33 U.S.C. 1251. 1998.

Georgia Environmental Protection Department. *An Overview of Redeployment.* 2000.

Earthjustice. *New Source Review: In the Shadows of Refineries: Communities Fighting for Clean Air.* Date not given.

Environmental Biosciences Program and Medical University of South Carolina *Environmental Justice: Strengthening the Bridge between Economic Development and Sustainable Communities.* 1999.

Federal Interagency Working Group and Medical University of South Carolina. *American Indian and Alaskan Native Environmental Justice Roundtable.* September 28, 2001.

GovExec.com. *EPA Stuck with Backlog of Environmental Justice Decisions,* News Brief. 2001.

Hazardous and Medical Waste Services Inc. *Public Involvement in Environmental Permits: An Action Plan.* 2001.

Higgins, Margot. *Poor Have Less Access to Clean Environment.* Environmental News Network. 2001.

Hill, Barry E. and Nicholas Targ. *The Link Between Protecting Natural Resources and the Issue of Environmental Justice.* Environmental Affairs. 2000. Available at http://www.epa.gov/commonsense/CSInews.html.

In re: Chemical Waste Management of Indiana, Inc. RCRA Appeal Nos 95-2 and 95-3 1995.

Interagency Environmental Justice Demonstration Project. *Re-Genesis: Cleanup and Revitalization through Collaborative Partnerships, Arkwright and Forest Park Community.* 2001.

Lazarus, Richard J. *Civil Rights in the New Decade: Highways and Bi-Ways for Environmental Justice.* Cumberland Law Review Symposium. 2001.

Louisiana Department of Environmental Quality. *Final Report to the Louisiana Legislature on Environmental Justice.* 1994.

Michigan Department of Environmental Quality, Governor's Office. *Draft Title VI Guidance for EPA Assistance Recipients Administering Environmental Permitting Programs: Draft Revised Guidance for Investigating Title VI Administrative Complaints.* 2000.

Miller, Maime. *Clean Air Act: Stationary Source Compliance Monitoring Strategy.* 2001.

Morgan Lewis, and Bockius LLP. *Environmental Justice Programs: 50-State Survey.* 2000.

National Environmental Justice Advisory Council. *A Regulatory Strategy for Siting and Operating Waste Transfer Stations—A Response to a Recurring Environmental Justice Circumstance: The Siting of Waste Transfer Stations in Low Income Communities and Communities of Color.* March 2000.

New York Public Interest Research Fund, Inc. and The Earth Day Coalition, Inc. *The Proof is in the Permit: How to Make Sure a Facility in Your Community Gets an Effective Title V Air Pollution Permit.* 2000.

O' Lone, Mary, Lawyer's Committee for Civil Rights Under Law. *Presentation for the National Academy of Public Administration Environmental Justice Panel.* 2001.

Public Law Institute at Hastings College of the Law. *Environmental Justice: A Review of State Responses.* 2000.

Safe Drinking Water Act. 42 U.S.C. 300f to 300j-26.

Shintech. *Community Response Document # 2 –Iberville Parish/West Baton Rouge Parish, Polyvinyl Chloride Manufacturing Facility.* 1999.

Tennessee Environmental Steering Committee and the Tennessee Department of Environment and Conservation. *Environmental Justice in the State of Tennessee.* 2000.

Texas Natural Resource Conservation Commission. *Guidance Package for Public Notification Procedures for New Source Review Air Quality Permit Applications.* 2001.

United States District Court for the District of New Jersey. *South Camden Citizens in Action v. New Jersey Department of Environmental Protection.* May 10, 2001.

U.S. Congress, House of Representatives. *Letter to Administrator Browner concerning Community Complaints and Disparate/Cumulative Impact.* 2000.

U.S. Department of Housing and Urban Development. *Empowerment Zones and Enterprise Communities Initiative (EZ/EC)* Available at http//www.hud.gov/progdesc/ezec.cfm/.

U. S. EPA. *Common Sense Initiative: An Industry Sector Approach for Protecting the Environment.* Available at http//www.epa.gov/commonsense/CSInews.html.

U. S. EPA. *Community Based Approaches.* 2000.

U. S. EPA. *Customer Service in Permitting: A Toolkit for Regions , States, and Local Permitting Authorities.* 1999. Available at http//www.epa.gov/customerservice/permits/.

U.S. EPA. *Draft Public Involvement Policy.* 2000.

U. S. EPA. *Environmental Permitting Clearinghouse.* 2001. Available at http//www.epa.gov/permits /.

U. S. EPA. *Interim Environmental Justice Policy.* 2001.

U. S. EPA. *Issues Regarding the Implementation of the Environmental Justice Executive Order Under the Prevention of Significant Deterioration (PSD) of Air Quality Regulations.* 1999.

U. S. EPA. *New Jersey Pushes Voluntary Approach to Environmental Justice Despite Court Ruling on State Inadequacies, Web News Brief.* 2001.

U. S. EPA. *The Next Generation in Permitting*. 1999. Available at http//www.epa.gov/permits/papmem.htm.

U. S. EPA. *Project XL—Encouraging Innovation, Delivering Results*. 2000.

U.S. EPA. *RCRA Expanded Public Participation Rule*. 1996.

U. S. EPA. *Region II Environmental Justice Analysis for Caribbean Petroleum and Refining L.P., Bayam'on, Puerto Rico*. 2001.

U. S. EPA. *Region II Environmental Justice Analysis for the Puerto Rico Aqueduct and Carolina Sewer Authority Regional Wastewater Treatment Plant*. 2000.

U. S. EPA. *Region V Interim Guidelines for Identifying and Addressing A Potential Environmental Justice Case*. 1998.

U. S. EPA. *Region IX Environmental Justice Assessment*. 1996.

U. S. EPA, Office of the Chief Financial Officer. *Strategic Plan*. 2000.

U. S. EPA Office of Cooperative Environmental Management. *National Advisory Council for Environmental Policy and Technology (NACEPT)—Incentives to Promote Environmental Stewardship*. 1999.

U. S. EPA, Office of Environmental Policy Innovation. *Evaluating the Environmental Justice Collaborative Model*. 2001.

U.S. EPA, Office of Federal Activities. *Final Guidance for Incorporating Environmental Justice Concerns In NEPA Compliance Analyses*. 1998.

U.S. EPA, Office of Solid Waste and Emergency Response . *RCRA Public Participation Manual*. 1996.

U.S. EPA, Office of Solid Waste and Emergency Response. *Waste Transfer Stations— A Manual For Decision Making*. 2001.

U.S. EPA, Office of Solid Waste and Emergency Response. *Sensitive Environments and the Siting of Hazardous Waste Management Facilities*. 1997.

U.S. General Accounting Office. *Chemical Risk Assessment—Selected Federal Agencies' Procedures, Assumptions, and Policies*. GAO-01-810. 2001.